The *Good News* of *God's Mercy*

Luke

Kevin Perrotta

Gerald Darring

**Six Weeks
with the Bible
for Catholic Teens**

6

Exploring
God's Word

LOYOLAPRESS.

CHICAGO

LOYOLAPRESS.

3441 N. ASHLAND AVENUE
CHICAGO, ILLINOIS 60657
(800) 621-1008
WWW.LOYOLABOOKS.ORG

Nihil Obstat
Reverend Charles R. Meyer, S.T.D.
Censor Deputatus
January 13, 2004

Imprimatur
Most Reverend Edwin M. Conway, D.D.
Vicar General
Archdiocese of Chicago
January 14, 2004

The *Nihil Obstat* and *Imprimatur* are official declarations that a book is free of doctrinal and moral error. No implication is contained therein that those who have granted the *Nihil Obstat* and *Imprimatur* agree with the content, opinions, or statements expressed.

32–33 From Jack Dellorto's reminiscence which originally appeared in *God's Word Today* magazine.

56–57 From *On the Edge of the Primeval Forest* by Albert Schweitzer (London: A.C. Black, 1924).

Cover and Interior Design: Th!nk Design Group

ISBN 0-8294-2052-5

Printed in the United States of America
04 05 06 07 08 Bang 5 4 3 2 1

Contents

How to Use This Guide 4

The Purpose of Luke's Gospel—
and How to Connect with It 6

WEEK **1** **Surprised by God**
Luke 1:26–55. 12

WEEK **2** **An Argument About Dinner**
Luke 5:12–32. 24

WEEK **3** **A Man Had Two Sons**
Luke 15:1–3, 11–32 36

WEEK **4** **No Servant Can Serve Two Masters**
Luke 16:13–15, 19–31 48

WEEK **5** **You Will Be with Me in Paradise**
Luke 22:14–20, 24–30; 23:32–43 60

WEEK **6** **The Lord Has Risen Indeed**
Luke 24:13–35 72

After Words 82

Mercy and More Mercy 84

A Young Person's Gospel 88

Listening When God Speaks 92

Resources 95

How to Use This Guide

You might compare this booklet to a short visit to a national park. The park is so large that you could spend months, even years, getting to know it. But a brief visit, if carefully planned, can be worthwhile. In a few hours you can drive through the park and pull over at a handful of sites. At each stop you can get out of the car, take a short trail through the woods, listen to the wind blowing in the trees, and get a feel for the place.

In this booklet we'll travel through the Gospel of Luke. We will take a leisurely walk through our targeted readings, which have been chosen to give a representative sample of Luke's telling of the good news of Jesus Christ.

After each discussion we'll get back in the car and take the highway to the next stop. The "Between Discussions" pages summarize the portions of Luke that we will pass along the way.

This guide provides everything you need to explore the Gospel of Luke in six discussions—or to do a six-part exploration on your own. The introduction will prepare you to get the most out of your reading. The weekly sections feature key passages from Luke, with explanations that highlight what his words mean for us today. Equally important, each section supplies questions that will launch you into fruitful discussion, helping you both to explore Luke for yourself and to learn from one another. If you're using the booklet by yourself, the questions will spur your personal reflection.

Each discussion is meant to be a *guided discovery.*

Guided ~ None of us is equipped to read the Bible without help. We read the Bible *for* ourselves but not *by* ourselves. Scripture was written to be understood and applied in and with the Church. So each week "A Guide to the Reading," drawing on the work of both modern biblical scholars and Christian writers of the past, supplies background and explanations. The guide will help you grasp Luke's message. Think of it as a friendly park ranger who points out noteworthy details and explains what you're looking at so you can appreciate things for yourself.

Discovery ~ The purpose is for *you* to interact with Luke's Gospel—and with Jesus, whom Luke describes. "Questions for a Closer Look" is a tool to help you dig into the Gospel and examine it carefully. "Questions for Application" will help you discern what the Gospel means for your life here and now. Each week concludes with an "Approach to Prayer" section that helps you respond to God's Word. Supplementary "Living Tradition" and "Saints in the Making" sections offer the thoughts and experiences of Christians past and present in order to show you what the Gospel has meant to others—so that you can consider what it might mean for you.

If you are using this booklet for individual study, pay special attention to the questions provided for each week (Warm-Up Questions, Questions for a Closer Look, Questions for Application). One advantage of individual study is that you can take all the time you need to consider all the questions. I also suggest that you read the Gospel of Luke in its entirety; you will find that the "Between Discussions" pages will help you understand the portions of the Gospel not covered in this booklet. And take your time making your way through the Gospel of Luke and this accompanying booklet: let your reading be an opportunity for this Gospel to become God's words to you.

The Purpose of Luke's Gospel—and How to Connect with It

Life does not always go as smoothly as we would like, and sometimes we go through very bad times. Even young people experience tragedy and misfortune, profoundly moving and sad events that may cause them to question themselves, their lives, and God. If that ever happens to you, it might make you especially well prepared to read the Gospel of Luke, because you will have insight into an issue we face as we read this Gospel.

The issue is this: will I be able to succeed in life by using my talents and resources? Or do I see within myself sources of both failure and success? For example, do I tend to use my talents selfishly for myself, caring only about what's good for me and not caring about the needs of others? Do I think only about my achievements and ignore my failures to love? Is all my attention focused on what I can do in this world, or do I also reflect on my inevitable aging and death? In other words, do I see myself as a creature possessing both wonderful gifts and flaws and limitations?

None of us likes to face the things about ourselves that we can't change—our weaknesses, our tendencies toward evil, the fact that we will die. But the Gospel of Luke tells us that God has done something to help us. In the language of the Bible, God has brought us salvation: he has come to heal us completely, to rescue us from the evils that threaten us—to rescue us even from death. To benefit from what God has done for us, we must first recognize that we need God's help.

Luke's Gospel deals with the issue of being open to God's work through Jesus. Luke shows us that God has made salvation available through Jesus' birth, life, death, and resurrection. In many ways, God's action through Jesus was unexpected, even for the Jewish people of the time. The salvation Jesus brings goes far beyond what people were looking for. It also makes demands on those who accept it. So we meet people in Luke's Gospel who are astonished by Jesus. They are struggling to understand what Jesus was offering them and how they should respond.

The people described in Luke's Gospel respond to Jesus in different ways, according to how much they recognize the need for God to intervene in their lives. Some people feel no need for what Jesus offers. They think they know where they stand with God, where they are going in life, and how they are going to get there. They think they know themselves.

Others who meet Jesus are not so sure they have it all together. They recognize that they need something from Jesus, although they are not sure what it is. So they are willing to let God intervene in their lives through Jesus, even if it means being challenged in surprising ways.

We will be reading about religious leaders who are satisfied with themselves even though they lack compassion and are spiritually malnourished (Weeks 2 and 3). Jesus says to them sharply, "If you're so healthy, you don't need *my* medical services." If they had been more truthful with themselves, they might have approached Jesus with more of an open mind.

Then there are physically sick people who encounter Jesus (Week 2). They know they need *something,* and they hope that Jesus can provide it. They may not understand everything about their deepest needs and about Jesus, but at least they come.

The person we will meet who is most realistic about himself is a man who is executed on a cross next to Jesus (Week 5). He has no illusions about himself. He knows his crimes and sees his total need for God's mercy. This criminal is the only person in the Gospel who reaches out to accept the whole rescue from sin and death that God offers us in Jesus.

This booklet is titled *Luke: The Good News of God's Mercy.* All of us want to experience God's mercy, so we take up the reading of Luke with some awareness of why we need God's mercy. We know that something in ourselves and in our lives needs to be set right, forgiven, healed.

But are we ready to hear a different perspective on what is wrong with us, one that is less pleasant than our own? Can we put aside for a while our own ideas about who we are, where our lives should be going, and what our needs truly are? Are we willing to admit that perhaps we do not know ourselves all that well?

This is what we do when there is something wrong with us physically. We know where it hurts but we don't know what is wrong or how it should be treated. So we go to a doctor, who can tell us what the problem is and what we need to do about it. What happens when our reading brings us in contact with Jesus, the physician par excellence?

Luke will show us that sometimes the thing that people need most is to have their eyes opened to what they really need. They may not recognize their lack of compassion or their unwillingness to serve others. In fact, their practice of religion may hide the problem from them. Do we see anything of this in ourselves?

God may give us not only a surprising diagnosis but also a surprising remedy. Jesus does not ignore what we feel is the problem. When a person with a skin disease comes to Jesus, Jesus heals his skin disease. When a paralyzed man is brought to Jesus, Jesus restores his ability to walk. Jesus shares our concerns about our problems, but he understands that we need to do more than just get favors from God. We need to put more effort into serving God and the people around us. God's mercy comes to take hold of us and fit us into *his* plans, which may be different from the plans we have for ourselves. God has more in mind for us than we expect when he heals us. Are we willing to have our expectations exceeded?

In the Gospel of Luke, we make contact with a will other than our own. God shows that he is not a spectator-god who made a DVD of the universe billions of years ago and now sits back to watch. God has a loving plan; God makes things happen. It is this active, involved God who comes to Mary and tells her about his plan for her in Luke's Gospel. As we begin reading the Gospel of Luke, are we prepared to meet this God?

So far, we have been looking at Luke's Gospel from the perspective of a tourist, accompanied by a tour guide who suggests the best position from which to look at a site: "Stand over here to get the best view!" But let us also take a few minutes to focus on Luke's Gospel itself. Now that we are in an appropriate position from which to view Luke's Gospel, what do we see?

Luke's Gospel is an account in eight parts. Luke has not marked the sections with subheads or chapter titles. All of the headings (and even the chapter and verse numbers) have been added by translators and editors to help us find our way through the text. Ancient authors used other headings, but this is the order that scholars now think we should note in the text:

1. Prologue (1:1–4) ~ Luke tells us briefly why he is writing. We won't discuss the prologue, but it takes just a few seconds to read.

2. Birth (1:5—2:52) ~ Luke tells two stories, the coming of Jesus and the coming of John the Baptist, who played an important role in introducing Jesus' ministry. By telling us the stories of their births side by side, Luke makes it easy for us to see how they are alike and how they are different. One way they are alike is that the angel Gabriel announced the conception of both boys. This makes it clear that they both are part of God's plan to rescue and restore us. One way they are different is that the angel makes the announcement to John's father, but to Jesus' mother. Jesus, after all, does not have a human father. God is Jesus' Father, so Jesus is God's Son. The text for Week 1 comes from this section.

3. Preparation (3:1—4:13) ~ John calls the people to repentance, and this sets the scene for Jesus to appear. John baptizes Jesus, who, filled with God's Spirit, undergoes a test of his trust and obedience toward God. In its own way this section also presents Jesus as God's Son. We won't be discussing anything from this section, but the "Between Discussions" pages will say more about it.

4. Ministry in Galilee (4:14—9:50) ~ Jesus walks from village to village, announcing the fulfillment of God's plan for meeting our deepest needs. He heals people to show that his message is true and that God's plan is all about giving us life. His wonderful deeds also point to the central role Jesus played in doing God's work.

Jesus teaches people how to respond to what God is doing, gathers a group of followers, and makes some enemies. The reading for Week 2 helps us understand this period of Jesus' life— a time when his words and works make people wonder, "Who is this man?" The section ends in a double climax. Jesus' followers recognize that he is indeed the one who will bring God's salvation. Then they see a vision in which God himself says of Jesus, "This is my Son, my chosen. Listen to him!"

5. A long trip (9:50—19:27) ~ Once Jesus' followers recognize who he is, he begins a long journey to Jerusalem. He knows that in Jerusalem he will enter into glory and authority with God, but he will do so in a way that seems unimaginable to his followers—death on a cross. On his way toward this suffering, Jesus spends his time teaching people about God's mercy and about how God wants them to be merciful. Weeks 3 and 4 offer samples of this teaching.

It is significant that Jesus teaches as he travels. Jesus gives his instructions as he walks along the road to show that he is not just interested in our following directions. He wants us to follow him personally, just as his disciples followed him on the road to Jerusalem.

6. Ministry in Jerusalem (19:28—21:38) ~ Jesus enters the city like a king and takes his stand as a teacher in the Temple. Luke helps us see that everything Jesus does and teaches shows him to be God's Son, the one who will bring salvation.

7. Death (22:1—23:56) ~ Jesus has come to
Jerusalem expecting to die, so he allows a plot to develop against
him. On the night his enemies have chosen, he deliberately waits
for them to come and seize him. He is convinced that his death
must happen; it is the way designated by God for him to enter
into eternal kingship and thus to bring God's salvation into the
world. Before his death, he and his followers eat a meal that is
heavy with meaning. As he dies, he makes it clear in a
conversation with a fellow dying man why he is dying. We will
read about these moving and profound episodes in Week 5.

8. Resurrection (23:56—24:53) ~ Three days
after Jesus' death, his friends discover that his tomb is empty.
Then, from his new position of eternal kingship and glory, Jesus
appears to his followers. He helps them understand how he will
continue to be among them (Week 6). In a final appearance,
Jesus guides his followers toward the next stage of God's plan
for them, which Luke discusses in his second volume, the Acts
of the Apostles.

So much for introduction. After the tour bus has arrived at
a historical site, and the guide has suggested a suitable vantage
point, and we have heard an explanation of the place's
significance, comes the reason why we made the journey:
we get to see for ourselves. Let us begin to read Luke carefully
and attentively, asking the Holy Spirit to bring Luke's words
alive as God's words to us.

Surprised by God

Warm-Up Questions

1 Reflect for a moment on which of these describes best the way you feel right now:
- ○ I like the way things are going in my life.
- ○ My life is fine, except for this one thing.
- ○ I would love to change a lot of things in my life.

2 Do you like surprises in your life, or would you prefer for things to proceed as expected?

3 Can you think of a time when something unexpected happened, and it turned out to be a blessing from God?

4 Where do you need God's help most right now: at school? at home? with friends? in your personal life?

Opening the Bible

What's Happened

In the Gospel's first episode (1:5–25), Luke relates an incident involving an elderly priest named Zechariah who worked at the Jewish Temple in Jerusalem. God sent an angel to Zechariah to tell him that his wife, Elizabeth, who was also no longer young, would soon bear a child—her first. When this child grows up, he will become known as John the Baptist and will prepare people to follow Jesus.

THE READING

Luke 1:26–55

A Very Unexpected Announcement

^{1:26} The angel Gabriel was sent by God to a town in Galilee called Nazareth, ²⁷ to a virgin engaged to a man whose name was Joseph, of the house of David. The virgin's name was Mary. ²⁸ And he came to her and said, "Greetings, favored one! The Lord is with you." ²⁹ But she was much perplexed by his words and pondered what sort of greeting this might be.

³⁰ The angel said to her, "Do not be afraid, Mary, for you have found favor with God. ³¹ And now, you will conceive in your womb and bear a son, and you will name him Jesus. ³² He will be great, and will be called the Son of the Most High, and the Lord God will give to him the throne of his ancestor David. ³³ He will reign over the house of Jacob forever, and of his kingdom there will be no end."

³⁴ Mary said to the angel, "How can this be, since I am a virgin?"

³⁵ The angel said to her, "The Holy Spirit will come upon you, and the power of the Most High will overshadow you; therefore the child to be born will be holy; he will be called Son of God. ³⁶ And now, your relative Elizabeth in her old age has also conceived a son; and this is the sixth month for her who was said to be barren. ³⁷ For nothing will be impossible with God."

³⁸ Then Mary said, "Here am I, the servant of the Lord; let it be with me according to your word." Then the angel departed from her.

A Joyful Visit

³⁹ In those days Mary set out and went with haste to a Judean town in the hill country, ⁴⁰ where she entered the house of Zechariah and greeted Elizabeth. ⁴¹ When Elizabeth heard Mary's greeting, the child leaped in her womb. And Elizabeth was filled with the Holy Spirit ⁴² and exclaimed with a loud cry, "Blessed are you among women, and blessed is the fruit of your womb. ⁴³ And why has this happened to me, that the mother of my Lord comes to me? ⁴⁴ For as soon as I heard the sound of your greeting, the child in my womb leaped for joy. ⁴⁵ And blessed is she who believed that there would be a fulfillment of what was spoken to her by the Lord."

Mary Declares God's Greatness

⁴⁶ And Mary said,
"My soul magnifies the Lord,
⁴⁷ and my spirit rejoices in God my Savior,
⁴⁸ for he has looked with favor on the lowliness of his servant.
Surely, from now on all generations will call me blessed;
⁴⁹ for the Mighty One has done great things for me,
and holy is his name.
⁵⁰ His mercy is for those who fear him
from generation to generation.
⁵¹ He has shown strength with his arm;
he has scattered the proud in the thoughts of their hearts.
⁵² He has brought down the powerful from their thrones,
and lifted up the lowly;
⁵³ he has filled the hungry with good things,
and sent the rich away empty.
⁵⁴ He has helped his servant Israel,
in remembrance of his mercy,
⁵⁵ according to the promise he made to our ancestors,
to Abraham and to his descendants forever."

Questions for a Closer Look

1 If Mary is told in verse 30 not to be afraid, why does she talk about fear in verse 50?

2 Look at verses 35 and 41 and reflect on how the Holy Spirit works in our lives.

3 According to Mary's prayer, what will God do for
- those who fear him?
- the lowly?
- the hungry?
- his servant Israel?

4 Look at the different things that God is said to have done in verses 51–53. What do they tell you about the kind of God we believe in?

5 In a sentence or two, how would you sum up the central message of this week's reading?

A Guide to the Reading

Nazareth is today a sprawling working-class town of some 70,000 residents. In Mary's day, it was a mere cluster of stone houses, home to perhaps a couple of hundred people. A young woman is indoors, apparently alone, when suddenly an angel appears and addresses her (1:26–28). They have a short but important conversation. By the time the angel leaves, the most important event in history is under way. It has been launched in a village so obscure that it is not mentioned in any records of the time. It has been launched through a seemingly insignificant young woman who was probably still in her early teens.

The angel does not tell Mary exactly what God has in store for her son. But clearly this Jesus will play a decisive part in God's plan. God will use Jesus to change for good the way he relates to us, for Jesus will reign "forever" (1:33). Up until then God had helped people in various, somewhat indirect, ways (see Hebrews 1:1). Now he is sending a "special agent" to deal face-to-face with our ills. The angel uses the language of kingship to show that Jesus will receive authority (1:32–33). Jesus is God's Son, conceived by the Spirit, so he will be God's personal representative. Indeed, in Jesus, God is coming in person.

The child is the center of attention, but we cannot help noticing the mother also. What a difference between God's magnificent plan and the humble young girl living in Nazareth!

Yet God does not overwhelm her. Gabriel's words show how highly God respects her. She is the only person in the entire Bible to be greeted as "favored one." This simple greeting—in 1:28—marked the person most favored by God, and it was reserved for Mary alone. On other occasions when an angel announced the birth of a child, the dialogue would end after the heavenly messenger gave a final reassurance (for example, 1:20). In Mary's case, the messenger waits for her to say yes (1:38).

All this demonstrates that God is not *using* Mary; he is commissioning her for the important task of raising his Son. He has chosen her for this responsibility (preserving her from sin from her conception, as the Church believes), and he seeks her cooperation. Mary thinks, questions, and then gives herself freely to God's plan. She acknowledges that she is God's servant— literally, in the Greek, his slave—a person who belongs to him fully.

The angel tells Mary that her older relative Elizabeth has unexpectedly become pregnant, so Mary goes to visit her. Elizabeth will be someone with whom Mary can share her extraordinary experience.

Elizabeth lived roughly 90 miles south of Nazareth, and the trip would have taken Mary four days or more. When Mary arrives, God inspires Elizabeth to recognize the child that Mary is now carrying (1:41–43). Notice that Elizabeth congratulates Mary not only for being chosen to bear the Savior (1:42) but also for cooperating with God's plan (1: 45). In response, Mary sings God's praises (1:46–55).

These events give us, like they did Mary (1:29), plenty to think about. She experienced God as having a surprising plan for her life, who intervened at the moment of his choosing, who valued her immensely. It is true that God's plan for Mary was unique, but we too are in a relationship with this God of surprises. What does this mean for us? To Mary, God revealed his intention to make himself present in the midst of ordinary human circumstances. Do we see God's presence in the simple and ordinary events of our lives?

Elizabeth and Mary rejoice (1:41–55). All of us would like to have more joy in our lives, but where can we find it? This reading suggests that the source of joy is experiencing God's loving action toward us. The question we need to ask ourselves, then, is whether we understand that these events in Luke's Gospel are God's actions *for us.*

Questions for Application

1 Mary takes a risk when she says yes to God's plan. Think of the risks that teenagers often take. Which of those risks are productive in their lives? Which are counter-productive, even destructive?

2 Mary talks about God, but she also talks about the great things God has done for her. How do you feel when people talk about themselves? Do you think people should be honest about their strengths as well as their weaknesses?

3 Think of something that did not go the way you expected. What did you learn from the experience?

4 What does today's reading teach us about what is important to God? about what God wants to accomplish? about how God relates to people? Does this sound like the kind of God you would like to know and talk with? How might this picture of God help you at this point in your life?

5 God calls on Mary to play a servant role in his plans. What service to others do you think God has in mind for you? How will it affect your life if you say yes to God's challenge?

6 How do people show mercy to each other? Is there someone in your family or your circle of friends who is a good example of a merciful person? What can you learn from that person?

Approach to Prayer

The first two joyful mysteries of the Rosary are the Annunciation (Gabriel's announcement to Mary) and the Visitation (Mary's visit to Elizabeth). Pray these two decades of the Rosary aloud with the group.

Then, if you wish, share with the group a blessing for which you are especially grateful.

A Living Tradition

Hail, Mary

The Hail Mary that we recite in the Rosary comes from today's reading.

"Hail, Mary, full of grace! The Lord is with you!" comes from Gabriel's greeting in 1:28 (as it was rendered in an old Latin translation).

"Blessed are you among women, and blessed is the fruit of your womb" comes from Elizabeth's congratulations to Mary in 1:42. With Elizabeth, we congratulate Mary not only for her motherhood, but also for her response to God (1:45). Our congratulations imply a willingness on our part to imitate her.

Christians in the Middle Ages combined these passages and added the name "Jesus" as the fruit of Mary's womb.

When we go on to say, "Holy Mary, mother of God, pray for us sinners," we are seeking the grace to be able to respond in our lives through Jesus: "Let it be with me according to your word" (1:38).

Eventually the practice developed of linking 50 Hail Marys into a *rosarium,* or rose garden, the rose being a symbol of joy, and the prayer being a celebration of Mary's joy.

Today's reading also helps explain Catholic devotion to Mary and why we continue to greet and congratulate Mary in our prayers. Mary declares, "From now on all generations will call me blessed; for the Mighty One has done great things for me" (1:48–49). In effect, Mary was saying, "From now on people will remark about me, 'The Lord made her truly happy!'"

When we "hail" Mary and declare her truly happy, we remind ourselves where true happiness lies. Mary's happiness, and ours, lies in the God who revealed himself to her—the God who takes the initiative to intervene in human lives and save us.

Between Discussions

Mary leaves Elizabeth after a lengthy visit, and Elizabeth has her baby. Zechariah offers a prophetic prayer over their infant son (1:57–80).

Six months later, Mary again travels south, this time with Joseph, to the district where Zechariah and Elizabeth live. They are complying with a government census requirement. Mary and Joseph arrive in the town of Bethlehem (today a 20-minute drive from Jerusalem) in time for Mary to give birth. A prophetic song is also prayed over this child, but not by Joseph. At Jesus' birth, it is not an earthly father but angels who sing (2:8–14), reminding us that Jesus' Father is in heaven.

Luke only tells one story from the years between Jesus' infancy and his public life (2:41–52). By now it will come as no surprise that this boyhood episode underlines Jesus' relationship with God. Jesus' first recorded words affirm that he must be busy with his Father's business (or in his Father's house—the Greek text can be read either way).

Except for that incident, Luke passes over Jesus' life until Jesus is 30. We know only that Jesus grew up in Nazareth, presumably in a small house built on the dry hillside overlooking the green Jezreel Valley.

Suddenly, in the wilderness along the Jordan River, John the Baptist begins to preach. His preaching attracts large crowds (3:1–18). John announces that Israel's history is approaching its climax. God's people have gone astray in sin and are shortly headed toward a final showdown with God's justice. The only way for them to avoid the sentence God is about to pass on their lives is by turning their minds and hearts around. The Judge is already on the way!

Jesus seems to have taken John's preaching as the signal to leave Nazareth. He sets out southward to the place where John is preaching and is baptized by John (3:21). Afterward as Jesus prays, God confirms his special relationship with the Father: "You are my Son, the Beloved; with you I am well pleased" (3:22).

A period of prayer, fasting, and testing in the wilderness follow this event (4:1–13). The testing revolves around the question of whether Jesus will continue to act as God's Son, trusting and obeying his Father. Jesus passes the test and returns to Galilee.

By accepting John's baptism, Jesus showed that he agreed with John's message. Yet Jesus will now give his own twist to the message. John proclaimed that God's Kingdom was about to arrive; Jesus will proclaim that it is *arriving*.

In his very first homily, Jesus quotes an Old Testament prophecy about the coming of God's Kingdom and judgment. But if you compare Isaiah 61:2 and Luke 4:19, you will notice that Jesus omits the line about judgment. Jesus agrees with John that God's judgment is coming. But at present, Jesus declares, God's Kingdom is breaking into the world with mercy. To show that God's mercy is near, Jesus accompanies his preaching with healing.

Jesus and John both realize that sin cuts people off from God. But Jesus' approach to the problem is different from John's. John called people to repent so that they would be ready for God's coming Kingdom. Jesus brings God's Kingdom in order to lead people to repentance. The difference is seen in the way John and Jesus conduct themselves. John remains in the wilderness; those who repent go out to him to be baptized. Jesus comes to the towns and homes of people who have not yet repented, demonstrating God's love for them in order to lead them to repentance.

Mary had experienced God's intervention in her life when he blessed her with the gift of bearing and raising his Son. In the same way, the people who live in the small towns of Galilee will now experience God's initiative through Jesus.

An Argument About Dinner

Warm-Up Questions

1 At the start of a new school year
  ○ I talk with as many people as possible.
  ○ I spend most of my time with one or two friends.
  ○ I'm interested in making new friends.
  ○ I like renewing old acquaintances.
  ○ I stay away from big groups.

2 What ingredients make for a successful celebration such as a birthday party or a wedding reception? What could detract from the success of a celebration? What was the happiest celebration you ever took part in?

3 In what situations might a young person feel left out? How might he or she deal with those situations?

4 How would you react if God gave you something different from what you asked for?

Opening the Bible

What's Happened

Some 30 years have passed, and Jesus has now begun his public activity.

The main thing he has done so far has been to give a kind of keynote address at Nazareth. The time has arrived, he said, when God would release the poor, the imprisoned, and the sick— through him (4:16–21). His fellow villagers seemed delighted that one of their own was going to play such a prominent role in God's plans (4:22). One can picture the chamber of commerce members already preparing the sign: "Welcome to Nazareth, childhood home of Jesus the Wonder-Worker." But then Jesus made it clear that his mission would not provide any special advantages for his hometown (4:23–27), and this provoked a riot. Jesus narrowly escaped being lynched (4:28–30).

As the Gospel unfolds, we see that Jesus has not come to bring glory to his hometown, nor to make his disciples rich and powerful, nor to uphold the prerogatives of society's leaders, nor even to preserve his own life. He has come simply to show God's mercy to those who need it.

THE READING

Luke 5:12–32

Bringing a Man Back into the Community

5:12 Once, when he was in one of the cities, there was a man covered with leprosy. When he saw Jesus, he bowed with his face to the ground and begged him, "Lord, if you choose, you can make me clean." 13 Then Jesus stretched out his hand, touched him, and said, "I do choose. Be made clean." Immediately the leprosy left him. 14 And he ordered him to tell no one. "Go," he said, "and show yourself to the priest, and, as Moses commanded, make an offering for your cleansing, for a testimony to them."

15 But now more than ever the word about Jesus spread abroad; many crowds would gather to hear him and to be cured of their diseases. 16 But he would withdraw to deserted places and pray.

"Pardon Me for Dropping in Like This"

[17] One day, while he was teaching, Pharisees and teachers of the law were sitting near by (they had come from every village of Galilee and Judea and from Jerusalem); and the power of the Lord was with him to heal. [18] Just then some men came, carrying a paralyzed man on a bed. They were trying to bring him in and lay him before Jesus; [19] but finding no way to bring him in because of the crowd, they went up on the roof and let him down with his bed through the tiles into the middle of the crowd in front of Jesus. [20] When he saw their faith, he said, "Friend, your sins are forgiven you." [21] Then the scribes and the Pharisees began to question, "Who is this who is speaking blasphemies? Who can forgive sins but God alone?" [22] When Jesus perceived their questionings, he answered them, "Why do you raise such questions in your hearts? [23] Which is easier, to say, 'Your sins are forgiven you,' or to say, 'Stand up and walk'? [24] But so that you may know that the Son of Man has authority on earth to forgive sins"—he said to the one who was paralyzed—"I say to you, stand up and take your bed and go to your home." [25] Immediately he stood up before them, took what he had been lying on, and went to his home, glorifying God. [26] Amazement seized all of them, and they glorified God and were filled with awe, saying, "We have seen strange things today."

Eating with the Wrong Sort of People

[27] After this he went out and saw a tax collector named Levi, sitting at the tax booth; and he said to him, "Follow me." [28] And he got up, left everything, and followed him. [29] Then Levi gave a great banquet for him in his house; and there was a large crowd of tax collectors and others sitting at the table with them. [30] The Pharisees and their scribes were complaining to his disciples, saying, "Why do you eat and drink with tax collectors and sinners?" [31] Jesus answered, "Those who are well have no need of a physician, but those who are sick; [32] I have come to call not the righteous but sinners to repentance."

Questions for a Closer Look

1 Even though Jesus orders the man not to tell anyone about his healing (verse 14), the man seems not to have obeyed (verse 15). Why do you think he was so anxious to talk about the healing?

2 When the religious leaders insist that only God can forgive sins (verse 21), does Jesus agree or disagree with them? Does verse 24 help to answer the question?

3 How do you explain verse 23? Surely Jesus did not believe that it is actually easier to *say* "Your sins are forgiven" than "Stand up and walk." So what point is he making?

4 What do the religious leaders criticize Jesus for in verses 21 and 30? Do you think they were among those who praise God for Jesus' action (verse 26)?

5 What do verses 29 and 30 tell us about who was present at the dinner party, and who seems not to be present?

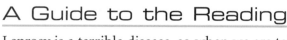

A Guide to the Reading

Leprosy is a terrible disease, so when we are told in the first episode that the man has leprosy, we focus our attention on his physical condition (5:12–14). But he probably was not suffering from what modern science calls leprosy, or Hansen's disease. Scholars think he probably had some kind of skin disease— psoriasis, for example.

Under the Jewish law, people with skin diseases were ritually impure and were to be kept apart from other people. This social aspect of the man's problem was what bothered him most: he asks Jesus to *cleanse* rather than *heal* him. He wants Jesus to cleanse him from ritual impurity (5:12). And notice that Jesus sends him to be checked out not by a doctor but by a priest, since only a priest could let him back into ordinary society by certifying that the ritual impurity was gone (5:14).

The incident, then, is about a man who wants to regain his normal place in society—and what Jesus does to fulfill that desire.

The typical Galilean house had a flat roof reached by an exterior stairway. So the paralyzed man's friends in the second episode (5:17–26) did not have to be acrobats to perform the feat in 5:19— although it took some nerve to take their neighbor's roof apart!

The paralyzed man must have believed Jesus could heal him. But he receives something different from what he expects (5:20). In Jesus' view, the man's main problem is not paralysis, but a broken relationship with God. So Jesus forgives his sins first, and only then does he heal the man's body. He shows his power to grant forgiveness (5:24) and to show compassion for the man. Did the paralyzed man realize that his sins were a greater problem than his paralysis? Was he at first disappointed by what Jesus did for him? He must have had a lot to think about afterward.

Levi (5:27–32) was technically a toll collector, someone whose job was to collect taxes for the government on goods transported on the roads. Toll collectors made a handsome profit by collecting more than they had to—a practice that did not make them popular. Nothing suggests that Levi was different from other tax collectors. At least, he seems to have had a lot of friends in the trade (5:29).

Men and women who valued justice shunned people like Levi. Jesus was concerned about justice, but he was concerned about Levi too. When he passed Levi on the road, Jesus did not ignore him, as most people would. Jesus looked at Levi carefully and spoke with him. Jesus went so far as to invite Levi to become one of his followers. (We can imagine how the other disciples felt about having to share a motel room with a tax collector!)

Levi throws a party in Jesus' honor with all the wrong kinds of people, and the religious leaders are astonished. The leaders practice a kind of holiness by dissociation (*Pharisee* means "separated one"). If Jesus is a representative of God, they want to know why he would associate with such disreputable people (5:30).

Jesus replies that God cannot wait for tax collectors and other unjust people to come to their senses. Sick people can't heal themselves; they need a doctor. God has sent his Son to be with those who oppose God, in order to draw them back into relationship with him (5:31–32).

Jesus, in other words, does not make people repent before they can be his friends. He offers people his friendship, hoping it will lead to repentance.

So everything Jesus does has to do with relationships. By touch, word, and friendship, he mends people's relationships with God and with one another.

Questions for Application

1 What can we learn from the leper's way of approaching Jesus in 5:12?

2 Are there any "lepers" in your school, students whom no one wants to be around? How should you relate to them? How could you improve the way you relate to them?

3 "Ritual impurity" meant that a person had a condition that made others want to stay away from him or her. Perhaps you know of some classmates or other students who have physical or other kinds of disabilities, and people prefer to stay away from them. What is something you can do to help students with special obstacles gain acceptance in the school?

4 Think of the biggest problem you have in your life right now. Suppose Jesus were to tell you that something else was really your biggest problem. How might you react? Would it change the way you relate to him?

5 Shouldn't teenagers be careful about with whom they hang around? Isn't it a problem when a young person mixes with the wrong crowd? What do you think of the example that Jesus gives in verses 29–32?

6 Are there any "tax collectors and sinners" at your school? How do you relate to them? How could you relate to them better?

Approach to Prayer

The friends of the paralyzed man brought him to the Lord and asked the Lord to satisfy their friend's greatest need. Spend a few moments thinking of all your friends, and then silently say a prayer for their needs. Close by praying the Our Father aloud with the group.

——— or ———

When you discussed how Jesus treated the man with leprosy and the tax collectors, perhaps you thought of such people as those with AIDS, the mentally ill, or criminals, or perhaps you thought of some people you know personally. Pray for them now. If you wish, offer aloud a brief prayer for those people you are thinking of—and for help in relating to them in a caring, constructive way. End by praying the Our Father aloud with the group.

Saints in the Making

Paralyzed by Guilt

Jack Dellorto of Sarasota, Florida, was "paralyzed" after his 20-year-old son, James Anthony, died in an auto accident. He felt guilty, as though he had somehow failed his son. He was sure that if he had been a more loving father, his son never would have died. He even had dreams in which his son begged him for help. Jack was a psychiatric social worker, so he knew that his guilt feelings did not make any sense, but he could not get rid of them. And he was too ashamed to talk with anyone about them.

One Saturday he went to a Scripture workshop. He listened to a reading of the story of Jesus healing a paralyzed man, and then he was supposed to discuss a personal crisis with another participant. His personal crisis, of course, was his son Jim, but he talked about something else with his partner, a nice woman in her 50s. She then told him about something she had kept to herself: she had found a lump in her breast and was waiting for word on whether or not it was cancer. Her mother, sister, and several aunts had died of breast cancer, so she was terrified. Jack was moved by her openness, so he started telling her about Jim. She responded with compassion and understanding.

The group then reread the Gospel passage. This time the passage took on a new, more personal dimension for Jack. He began to feel healed of the paralysis of his grief. He would still mourn Jim, but now he was at peace with his son's death.

Jack has this to say about his healing:

God's generous grace directed me to "pick up my mat" of worries, repented sin, guilt, and everything else that paralyzed me—and get on with my life. I believe it also helped me to become more compassionate and empathetic. I now carry a different "mat": one of loving forgiveness, hope, and peace.

Between Discussions

Our second reading has let us see Jesus at work in rural Galilee. For some months Jesus remains in Galilee, continuing to heal sick people and teach about the Kingdom of God (for example, see 9:11). He invites others, like Levi, to accompany him as he walks from village to village.

The Kingdom that Jesus announces cannot be described in a single statement. Basically, it has to do with God becoming involved in our affairs. Jesus brings out different aspects of the Kingdom at different moments. In one sense the Kingdom is the world to come, when God will enable human beings to live in justice and happiness at the end of time (13:28–29). In this sense the Kingdom is coming soon (9:27), although not necessarily right away (19:11). But the Kingdom is also God's merciful care for human beings in the present world. We can see signs of it already springing up in Jesus' activities (17:20–21). These workings of the Kingdom are small-scale; the Kingdom is so powerful that it will eventually affect the entire world (13:18–21).

Kingdom of God can also be translated "reign of God." God's reign is a matter of God's action. Thus Jesus never asks people to *build* the Kingdom. God establishes it by his own power. Rather, Jesus challenges us to *enter* the Kingdom that God is bringing (18:24–25).

Jesus gives more signs that God has appointed him as the principal agent of the Kingdom. He calms a storm (8:22–25), restores the life of a girl who has died (8:49–56), and creates enough bread and fish to feed more than 5,000 people (9:10–17). The disciples wonder, Who *is* this man? The readers of the Gospel have been told about Jesus' origins and his designation by an angel as God's Son, but the disciples have not. They have to work out the answer to the question for themselves.

Jesus calls a time-out from preaching and healing to give his followers an opportunity to reflect on who he is (9:18). Peter, the leader among the disciples, tells Jesus what they have decided:

"You are the Messiah"—God's specially chosen agent of salvation (9:20). Jesus tells them to keep it to themselves (9:21), perhaps because they do not yet understand how he will carry out his role.

Jesus is working wonders and attracting favorable attention, so his disciples do not expect him to run into opposition from the religious leaders. Jews did not expect the Messiah to be rejected. Yet in our second reading (5:21,30) we have seen how the religious leaders in rural Galilee were not happy.

Jesus announces that God is going to take action that goes beyond the framework of the relationship that God set up with Israel through Moses. This new action is not against Israel. On the contrary, Jesus directs his ministry to his fellow Jews. He chooses exactly 12 close disciples as a sign that he wants to restore Israel as God's people. (Twelve was the number of the tribes of Israel.) Nevertheless, some aspects of the Jewish religion will no longer be as important as before. God's new action will cross the boundaries between Israel and the other nations of the world. The Temple in Jerusalem will no longer be the only place where God is present with his people. Naturally, there are some who do not like Jesus' version of the restored Israel because they like things the way they are. The existing system is working well for them. These religious leaders consider Jesus a pretender, arrogantly claiming to be God's unique, fully authorized agent (see 5:20–21).

Jesus warns his followers that the road ahead will not always be lined with admiring crowds (9:22). But they do not understand what this means for them.

Without waiting for them to understand, Jesus ends his work in Galilee and sets off toward Jerusalem, where he knows he will suffer (9:51). The journey turns out to be a long one (stretching from chapter 9 to chapter 19). Along the way, Jesus pauses to engage in the conversation with local religious leaders that is recounted in our next reading.

A Man Had Two Sons

Warm-Up Questions

1 Where do you fall in the birth order of children in your family? What difference might it have made if you had been born somewhere else in the order?

2 How easy do you think it is for young people to leave home? How do their families usually respond?

3 How should you react once you realize you have made a big mistake? How should you not react?

4 In what ways are you like your parents? In what ways are you different from them?

Opening the Bible

What's Happened

Our third reading seems to take up just where the second one left off: some of the religious leaders and Jesus are still discussing his friendship with well-known sinners. In fact, a great deal has happened in the meantime. After teaching, healing, disputing with religious leaders, and gathering disciples, Jesus has left Galilee and is now on his way south to Jerusalem.

The continuing debate over Jesus' dining in the homes of tax collectors and sinners shows that this practice was an important feature of his public life. Earlier Jesus used the analogy of a physician to explain his approach. In this reading, he tells an extended parable.

THE READING

Luke 15:1–3,11–32

The Griping About Jesus' Social Life Continues

¹⁵:¹ Now all the tax collectors and sinners were coming near to listen to him. ² And the Pharisees and the scribes were grumbling and saying, "This fellow welcomes sinners and eats with them." ³ So he told them this parable: . . .

A Headstrong Young Man

¹¹ "There was a man who had two sons. ¹² The younger of them said to his father, 'Father, give me the share of the property that will belong to me.' So he divided his property between them.¹³ A few days later the younger son gathered all he had and traveled to a distant country, and there he squandered his property in dissolute living. ¹⁴ When he had spent everything, a severe famine took place throughout that country, and he began to be in need. ¹⁵ So he went and hired himself out to one of the citizens of that country, who sent him to his fields to feed the pigs. ¹⁶ He would gladly have filled himself with the pods that the pigs were eating; and no one gave him anything.

^{17} But when he came to himself he said, 'How many of my father's hired hands have bread enough and to spare, but here I am dying of hunger! ^{18} I will get up and go to my father, and I will say to him, "Father, I have sinned against heaven and before you; ^{19} I am no longer worthy to be called your son; treat me like one of your hired hands."' ^{20} So he set off and went to his father. But while he was still far off, his father saw him and was filled with compassion; he ran and put his arms around him and kissed him. ^{21} Then the son said to him, 'Father, I have sinned against heaven and before you; I am no longer worthy to be called your son.' ^{22} But the father said to his slaves, 'Quickly, bring out a robe—the best one—and put it on him; put a ring on his finger and sandals on his feet. ^{23} And get the fatted calf and kill it, and let us eat and celebrate; ^{24} for this son of mine was dead and is alive again; he was lost and is found!' And they began to celebrate.

Not Everyone Is Pleased

^{25} "Now his elder son was in the field; and when he came and approached the house, he heard music and dancing. ^{26} He called one of the slaves and asked what was going on. ^{27} He replied, 'Your brother has come, and your father has killed the fatted calf, because he has got him back safe and sound.' ^{28} Then he became angry and refused to go in. His father came out and began to plead with him. ^{29} But he answered his father, 'Listen! For all these years I have been working like a slave for you, and I have never disobeyed your command; yet you have never given me even a young goat so that I might celebrate with my friends. ^{30} But when this son of yours came back, who has devoured your property with prostitutes, you killed the fatted calf for him!' ^{31} Then the father said to him, 'Son, you are always with me, and all that is mine is yours. ^{32} But we had to celebrate and rejoice, because this brother of yours was dead and has come to life; he was lost and has been found.'"

Questions for a Closer Look

1 Who is the central character in this story?

2 Notice the different ways the two brothers address their father (verses 12, 18, 21, 29). Notice also the different ways the older son and the father refer to the younger son (verses 30, 32). What do these differences tell us?

3 At whom is the older son angry?

4 Does the father disagree with the older brother's criticism of the younger brother's behavior (see verses 30, 32)?

5 The older brother accuses the father of being unfair. Is he?

6 In what ways are the two brothers alike?

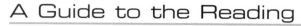

A Guide to the Reading

As in our last reading, the religious leaders criticize Jesus for mixing with people who have abandoned God's ways (see 5:29–30; 15:1–2). To use contemporary categories, it is as if the religious leaders are offended because Jesus is hanging around with drug dealers and makers of pornographic films.

Jesus answers them by telling a story that shows the depth of God's mercy—and challenges those who are not willing to be merciful. In a few words he describes a young man who is as selfish as he is stupid. The younger son wants to use his father to get what he wants, which is his inheritance. Dad, inconveniently, remains alive, but then he yields to his son's demand, and our young hero goes as far away from home as he can. He spends money freely without thinking about the future. Nevertheless, it is hard not to feel sorry for this boneheaded young man when his money runs out and friends are nowhere to be seen. He is reduced to feeding pigs—about as low as a Jewish boy can go.

The young man "came to himself" (5:17), although we may wonder whether he understands the depth of his sin. Is he really sorry for what he has done, or is he just doing what he has to in order to get food (5:17–19)?

Clearly he has miscalculated how much his father loves him. He cannot image that his father would receive him back into the family after what he has done. But the father has been watching the road for his son's return (see 5:20). The father *runs* to the son—not the kind of thing a respectable gentleman would do. He does not question his son to find out if he is really sorry. Before the son has finished his little speech, the father has already begun surrounding him with signs of acceptance: a robe, a ring, a reception. The father is more concerned about his son's honor than about his own!

Then there is the other son. He is off working in the fields when his good-for-nothing brother makes his appearance. Probably he would have been happier if his brother had *stayed* "lost" and "dead" (5:24,32). Yet he seems to be angry, not so much at his brother as at his father. The father has been unfair, he complains, welcoming the younger son home after making the older son slave away year after year without reward (5:29). Yet, is the older son right in portraying the father as demanding and stingy (see 5:31)? Or, in his own way, has the older son also miscalculated his father's love? Despite living under the same roof with his father, is he, too, "lost" and "dead"?

Standing outside the party, the older son is forced to make a decision. Will he also come to his senses? Jesus leaves the question unanswered. His listeners, the religious leaders, must answer the question with regard to themselves, for they are the real-life dutiful "older brothers." What do they think of the mercy that God is showing to his real-life wayward children?

For many of us, the older brother is the natural starting point for our reflections on Jesus' story, especially his attitude toward his father (5:29). He expresses something we sometimes feel but are reluctant to admit: God expects a lot and seems not to give much in return. This feeling obviously makes no sense, yet we feel it. It seems we need to hear the father's words (5:31) as God's answer to us.

Undoubtedly there are times, perhaps many times, when we identify with the younger brother. We all have a tendency to misuse God's gifts, and so we will get ourselves into messes and then we will have moments of coming to our senses. We will always need to be reminded about God's eagerness to forgive us.

Are we also willing to be like the father? Are we as anxious to forgive as we are to be forgiven? Will we not only receive compassion but also offer it to others?

Questions for Application

1 In what ways is the younger brother typical of many young people today? In what ways is he different? How might he be considered a role model for today's youth?

2 What are our usual motives for repenting of sin? Are they sometimes, or even always, mixed? Do you think this affects God's forgiveness?

3 Do you think that most people are unaware of how much God really loves them? How much are you aware? How might your awareness of God's love for you affect your relationship with others?

4 What issues would the younger son have to face after his return? What issues do you have to face after making up with a friend?

5 How would you characterize the older son? Are we all like him in some ways? Do we sometimes have to face a choice like the one he faced?

6 If you have children, would you like to be the kind of parent this father is? What do you think your biggest challenge would be in trying to imitate him?

Approach to Prayer

Listen as a member of the group offers a prayer for all the young people who are having difficulties with their parents. Pause for a few moments of reflection on your own relationship with your parents. Listen as another member of the group offers a prayer for parents.

Conclude with the Our Father.

or

Listen as members of the group pray aloud Psalms 51 and 103, which express repentance and confidence in God's mercy. Conclude with the Our Father.

A Living Tradition

The Purposes of the Parable

An encyclical is a letter issued by the pope for circulation among the bishops of the Church or among all the Catholic faithful. In 1980 the Holy Father, Pope John Paul II, issued an encyclical on the subject of the God of mercy. The letter included a section on the parable of the forgiving father.

Because the Holy Father was writing about God's mercy, he focuses most of his attention on the father in the story, but he does have things to say about the two sons. The younger son gained an inheritance, "but more important than these goods was his dignity as a son in his father's house." The humiliation that resulted from his loss of his material goods "should have made him aware of the loss of that dignity."

Eventually the young man comes to his senses and realizes that he has lost the "dignity that springs from the relationship of the son with the father." The father responds by being "faithful to his fatherhood, faithful to the love that he had always lavished on his son." He expresses that faithfulness by welcoming his son home and by joyful merrymaking.

The father knows that what has been saved is "the good of his son's humanity." In other words, the son had been close to losing his dignity as a human being, and the father has restored him to value as a human being. This, the Holy Father writes, is why the parable of the forgiving father "touches upon every breach of the covenant of love, every loss of grace, every sin." Our sins cause us to lose the dignity we have as children in our father's house, and when God shows us mercy and forgives us, "the person who is the object of mercy does not feel humiliated, but rather found again and 'restored to value.'"

This is precisely what Jesus did as Messiah: he restored our dignity as children of the Father. For that reason, writes Pope John Paul II, the mercy exemplified by the father of the prodigal son "constitutes the fundamental content of the messianic message of Christ."

Between Discussions

You may have noticed that our readings so far have all contained references to eating (1:53; 5:29–30; 15:16,23). Throughout Luke's Gospel there is plenty of eating and talk about eating. Many Gospel stories are about things that happen during meals in homes (7:36–50; 10:38–42; 14:7–24; 19:1–10). Jesus feeds more than 5,000 people with some bread and fish (9:10–17). He describes the Kingdom of God as a great banquet (14:15–24). On the night before he died, he gave his final instructions to his disciples during a meal (22:14–38). After his resurrection, he resumes his instructions and the conversation soon ends up at a dinner table (24:13–35).

It is hard for us to appreciate the meaning of all this dining. It is useful to slip on first-century glasses and see the eating in Luke's Gospel as it might have looked to people at the time.

For one thing, first-century people were much more concerned about getting enough to eat than we are today in our developed world. Before modern technology, there was simply less food to go around, and supplies were less certain. Many people lived at the subsistence level; that is, they were never far away from the possibility of starvation. Most people at one time or another really did not know where their next meal was coming from.

When Jesus miraculously fed thousands of people, it created a sensation in that hungrier first-century world. Here, indeed, was someone who could give people what they really needed! Here was someone with life-giving power! Nothing could have shown God's mercy more dramatically than a huge hillside banquet. No wonder it forms the climax of Jesus' miracles in Galilee.

Eating together was more important to first-century people than it is to us. We are often too busy to take the time to sit down with others and eat. We have a very casual attitude about eating our meals so we tend to miss the almost sacred importance that first-century people attached to meals. For them, eating with others expressed a bond with them—or it created one. Normally you ate at home with your family. If you ate out, it was likely to be in the home of a relative, friend, or patron, in a religious meeting place with fellow worshipers, or in the hall of a fraternal association. They would never have eaten meals with strangers, like we do in restaurants. If you did not have or want to have a relationship with someone, you would not eat with them. Thus, for example, Jews generally did not eat with non-Jews.

Now you can understand the reaction to Jesus' practice of dining with tax collectors and sinners. People who saw meals as sacred understood that Jesus was establishing a personal bond with people who had no use for justice and other moral values! He was telling us that God wants to have a friendly and faithful relationship with us without waiting for us to make the first move.

Some people, like Levi (5:27–28) and the tax collector Zacchaeus (19:1–10), dined with Jesus and experienced reconciliation with God and with his people. Gathering around the table with Jesus became an image of the restored community of God's people. In fact, a meal with Jesus was a foretaste of the banquet in the Kingdom of God. To dine at table with the king is to be already, in some sense, in his Kingdom.

Well, now we ourselves sit at table with Jesus when we celebrate the Eucharist. If we look at the Eucharist through first-century glasses, what features of the celebration stand out more clearly?

No Servant Can Serve Two Masters

Warm-Up Questions

1 When it comes to eating out
- ○ I like a touch of elegance.
- ○ Fast food is fine.
- ○ I like to try new restaurants.
- ○ Give me meat and potatoes, thanks.
- ○ Volume counts.

2 When have you volunteered your time to help a person or a cause? How was the experience rewarding? How was it frustrating?

3 What is your experience with homeless people in your town?

Opening the Bible

What's Happened

In our last reading, Jesus explained why he accepted dinner invitations from people who had turned their backs on God. The parable of the forgiving father conveyed the depth of God's love for sinful men and women. As the special agent of God's intervention in the world, Jesus showed this divine love through his friendships with people who rejected God. Jesus hoped to give them an experience of God's love for them.

The parable concluded with a challenge to us, the readers. As the story ended, the father in the story was pleading with his older son to come in to the celebration of his brother's return. This left us asking ourselves how we will relate to those who have turned away from God and have harmed other people. Will we be dominated by self-righteousness and resentment toward them? Or will we join with God and be compassionate representatives of his love?

Thus the parable of the forgiving father addressed one obstacle to our receiving God's merciful Kingdom: self-righteous judgmentalism. Now Jesus will focus on another obstacle: preoccupation with our own material advancement.

In the short portion of Luke between our reading last time and our reading today, Jesus urges his listeners to use their money to achieve heavenly, rather than earthly, happiness (16:1–8). Then he tells a story to show what it means to use material resources for heavenly ends. This story, with a few introductory remarks, is our reading for today.

THE READING

Luke 16:13–15,19–31

The Power of Money

16:13 "No slave can serve two masters; for a slave will either hate the one and love the other, or be devoted to the one and despise the other. You cannot serve God and wealth."

14 The Pharisees, who were lovers of money, heard all this, and they ridiculed him. 15 So he said to them, "You are those who justify yourselves in the sight of others; but God knows your

hearts; for what is prized by human beings is an abomination in the sight of God. . . .

A Rude Awakening

[19] "There was a rich man who was dressed in purple and fine linen and who feasted sumptuously every day. [20] And at his gate lay a poor man named Lazarus, covered with sores, [21] who longed to satisfy his hunger with what fell from the rich man's table; even the dogs would come and lick his sores.

[22] "The poor man died and was carried away by the angels to be with Abraham. The rich man also died and was buried. [23] In Hades, where he was being tormented, he looked up and saw Abraham far away with Lazarus by his side. [24] He called out, 'Father Abraham, have mercy on me, and send Lazarus to dip the tip of his finger in water and cool my tongue; for I am in agony in these flames.' [25] But Abraham said, 'Child, remember that during your lifetime you received your good things, and Lazarus in like manner evil things; but now he is comforted here, and you are in agony. [26] Besides all this, between you and us a great chasm has been fixed, so that those who might want to pass from here to you cannot do so, and no one can cross from there to us.'

[27] "He said, 'Then, father, I beg you to send him to my father's house—[28] for I have five brothers—that he may warn them, so that they will not also come into this place of torment.'
[29] Abraham replied, 'They have Moses and the prophets; they should listen to them.' [30] He said, 'No, father Abraham; but if someone goes to them from the dead, they will repent.' [31] He said to him, 'If they do not listen to Moses and the prophets, neither will they be convinced even if someone rises from the dead.'"

Questions for a Closer Look

1 In verses 24 and 27 the rich man treats Lazarus as someone who might be sent to run errands—as a social inferior. Why is the rich man still relating to Lazarus this way?

2 Would the story work if the rich man had not known Lazarus during their earthly life? Are there any signs in the story that he did know Lazarus?

3 Relate verse 15 to the story: What did the rich man prize? Was it "an abomination in the sight of God"? Why?

4 How would you briefly sum up the message—or messages— of the story?

A Guide to the Reading

If the story of the forgiving father is one of Jesus' most consoling parables, the story of the rich man and Lazarus is one of his most alarming. The young son returns home to be wined and dined. The rich man lands in a fiery pit. Both end up being toasted—but in very different senses!

Yet the two stories have some things in common. Both speak of God's mercy. The first story illustrates God's mercy toward sinners, the second his mercy toward the poor and the sick. God loves Lazarus, so he reverses his situation. He lifts him up from lying hungry on the ground and places him next to Abraham at the heavenly banquet.

In both stories a character faces a choice about showing mercy. In the parable of the forgiving father, the older son had to choose whether to share his father's mercy toward his brother; in the parable of the rich man and Lazarus, the rich man had to choose whether to extend mercy to Lazarus.

The stories tell us about what happens when we refuse to pass on God's mercy to others. It is like standing outside a party, angry at the world rather than enjoying the music. It is like being burned. These are only images, of course. They should not be taken literally, but they should be taken seriously as indications of how unhappy it can make us when we fail to participate in the mercy that God is showing in the world.

Did the wealthy man deliberately ignore Lazarus's suffering? Apparently. When he notices Lazarus next to Abraham, he already knows his name (16:24). How could he not know him? Day after day Lazarus lay "at his gate"—right outside his front door (16:20).

Was the rich man totally self-centered, someone who cared only about himself? Probably not. Most likely he was a respected member of society. He must have had others with him when he feasted every day (16:19). His table would have been crowded with important people like him—people who could do him favors, whose good opinion it was useful to have. The way to gain a good reputation back then was by being a benefactor, so the rich man may even have been generous—to those who could do things for him in return. But there would have been no point in being generous to Lazarus. Lazarus was a nobody. He could never do the rich man any favors; he could not do anything to help the rich man's reputation. In one sense Lazarus was close to the rich man—just outside the door. In another sense he was a million miles away.

And that is just how Lazarus appears to the rich man after death (16:23). In earthly life the rich man distanced himself as far as he could from Lazarus, and after death he will remain forever at that distance (16:26). And since Lazarus has arrived in heaven (represented by Abraham), being at an infinite distance from Lazarus means being at an infinite distance from God.

Jesus tells the story of the rich man and Lazarus to show the power that wealth has over us. Jesus does not see money as something passive or neutral; it is a force that competes with God for our loyalty (16:13). Money exerts a powerful influence over us. If we let ourselves be dominated by it, it will close our hearts to God.

Of course, we may not notice how love of money is keeping us away from God. But we *can* see the effect of money's influence in our relationship with people in need. Compassion toward other people shows that you are open to God. The rich man, however, fails to take notice of Lazarus at his door, and this shows his blindness toward God. His devotion to wealth and his love of money have rendered him blind to both Lazarus and God.

For Jesus the issue is not how much money we have but how much our money controls us (16:13). How consumed are we with buying and enjoying material things? How much of our money—and time—do we spend on people who are in need? Jesus does not give us a formula to figure out how well we are doing. He presents the issue squarely—love of God or love of money? love of the needy or love of self?—and leaves us to examine ourselves and make our decisions. Hopefully we will choose more wisely than the rich man in the parable!

Questions for Application

1 How do you think Lazarus might appear at our doorstep in today's world? What would be an appropriate individual response to him? an appropriate community response?

2 Think of all the obstacles that get in the way of using our time and money to meet other people's needs (for example, being too busy, not knowing where to start, not having much money). What could be done to overcome at least one of these obstacles in order to be more generous with our talents or resources?

3 What do you think is the biggest challenge presented by this reading? Does it suggest some concrete action that you might take?

4 The rich man saw Lazarus's suffering without caring enough to help him. What are some steps we can take to keep that kind of callous attitude from developing in ourselves?

5 How could you support one another in responding to this reading? What might you be able to do as a group to respond to this reading?

6 The story ends by addressing the problem of knowing God's will but failing to respond to it. Why do we sometimes do that?

Approach to Prayer

If you wish, mention a need—for yourself or for others—that you would like to be remembered in prayer. Then take a few moments to reflect silently, and conclude with this prayer:

*Lord Jesus, give me eyes to see
those in need and a heart to have
compassion. Help me come to the aid
of the needy as you did. Make me
a channel of your mercy. Help me not to
treat money and possessions as more
important than other people.*

 or

Listen as members of the group read aloud Psalms 111 and 112, which speak of divine generosity and human generosity. Conclude with the Our Father.

Saints in the Making

A Life-Changing Story

In 1905, at the age of 30, Albert Schweitzer had become famous as both a theologian and a professional organist. Yet he was unsettled about his future. When he read a magazine article asking European doctors to work in central Africa, Schweitzer knew what he must do. He left his promising dual careers and put himself through medical school. In 1913, after raising funds, Schweitzer set up a clinic on the Ogowe River in present-day Gabon. Except for a brief period during World War I, he worked there until his death in 1965.

In a 1924 book, Schweitzer explained the thinking that led to his decision:

> *I read about the physical miseries of the natives in the virgin forests. And the more I thought about it, the stranger it seemed to me that we Europeans trouble ourselves so little about the great humanitarian task which offers itself to us. The parable of Dives* and Lazarus seemed to me to have been spoken directly at us! We are Dives, for, through the advances of medical science, we now know a great deal about disease and pain, and have innumerable means of fighting them. Out there in the colonies, however, sits wretched Lazarus, the coloured folk, who suffers from illness and pain just as much as we do, nay, much more, and has absolutely no means of*

---

* The unnamed wealthy man in Jesus' parable in Luke 16 is sometimes called Dives, the Latin word for *rich.*

*fighting them. And just as Dives sinned against the poor
man at his gate because, for want of thought, he never
put himself in his place and let his heart and conscience
tell him what he ought to do, so do we sin against the
poor man at our gate.*

Between Discussions

In our second reading we saw Jesus invite a tax collector named Levi to become one of his disciples. In other sections of Luke, Jesus invites a good number of men and women to be disciples.

Jesus' specific words to Levi were "Follow me" (5:27). Jesus spent his days walking from village to village. He did not have a place to train others or even to live in himself. So to study under Jesus meant literally following him. For this reason, Jesus' disciples had to leave everyone and everything behind. Peter and Andrew could hardly take their boat along as they followed Jesus to the next town.

There were others who were devoted to him, but he did not call them to follow him as disciples. They were part of the restored community of God that he was gathering around him. But they stayed at home and did not follow him along the roads of Galilee.

Luke wrote some decades after Jesus' death and resurrection. By the time Luke was writing, everyone who believed in Jesus could be a disciple because Jesus was now always present in the whole Christian community. You couldn't literally follow Jesus, of course, because he was no longer walking around Galilee.

Still, Luke thought it helpful to talk about being a discile in terms of *following*. So in his Gospel he emphasized the picture of Jesus traveling along the road with his disciples. Luke included considerable material in his Gospel that the other Gospel writers did not use, and much of this was inserted into Jesus' journey to Jerusalem (chapters 9–19). The result is that in Luke's Gospel, much of Jesus' ministry takes place on the road. It is as though Luke wants to show that if we are disciples of Jesus, we will experience the sorts of things that the first disciples experienced as they followed him: spending time with him, paying attention to what he does, having our lives drawn toward the destiny that he was traveling to in Jerusalem—his passage from death into risen life.

If disciples of Jesus still follow, they must also, in some way, leave behind. They must get rid of possessions and give to the needy because Jesus draws them into a close, trusting relationship with God as Father. To trust in the real God, we have to stop trusting in the false god—money.

Just as Jesus did not ask all his first friends to leave home and follow him on the road, so he does not intend all of us to give away all our possessions. (Some of us, however, join a religious order and do indeed leave everything behind.) But Jesus does call all of us to dethrone the false god money and use our resources and talents to help meet the needs of the poor.

Jesus makes this point through a parable about a wealthy farmer who is the opposite of what a disciple should be. The man trusts in money, and he uses his money for himself alone, without taking anyone else into account (12:13–21). According to Jesus, this man is a "fool" (12:20).

Jesus declares that God's kingdom will reverse the condition of the poor. This is one message of the parable of the rich man and Lazarus. Jesus makes the same point in a parable of a host who gives a great banquet. When the wealthy people whom he invites decline to attend, he fills the house with beggars and other social misfits (14:15–24).

But the poor do not have to wait for God's Kingdom to come in order to see things change for them. Jesus heals them and gives them food, showing that God is already beginning to change things for the needy in the *present* world. Jesus wants his disciples to be inspired by the prospect of better things for the poor so that they will do something about poverty here and now. When you yourselves give a dinner party, Jesus says, invite beggars and other social misfits (see 14:12–14). Thus Jesus tells the story of the rich man and Lazarus to spur his stay-at-home disciples to do what the rich man had failed to do—care for the needy person on the doorstep.

You Will Be with Me in Paradise

Warm-Up Questions

1 Which one of these expresses your feelings about saying good-bye?
○ Keep it short and sweet.
○ I try to say good-bye to each person.
○ I like a hug.
○ It can take hours. (Sometimes the most interesting conversations happen when you're saying good-bye!)
○ I'd rather not say good-bye.

2 What is the most memorable meal you have ever had? Why do you remember it so well?

3 Why do we sometimes join in making fun of someone? Why is it so hard not to join in?

Opening the Bible

What's Happened

Jesus' long trip to Jerusalem has ended. He has arrived in Jerusalem at the time of the Passover celebration.

Thousands of pilgrims have crowded into the city for the feast. Many have arrived a week before the feast begins so they can ritually purify themselves. Jesus picks this busy time to do something that was sensational and symbolic. He drives out some people who were carrying on business that was necessary for the Temple to function (19:45–48). He wants to clear away commercial activities in the Temple. But Jesus seems to be saying that, now that he has arrived on the scene, the Temple will no longer play a central role in God's relationship with his people. This brings Jesus into conflict with the priests in charge of the Temple.

Jesus teaches publicly in the Temple by day, and in the evenings he teaches on a nearby hillside with his disciples. Meanwhile the Temple authorities plot to arrest him and have him killed. Knowing what is afoot, Jesus shares a final meal with his inner circle of disciples.

THE READING

Luke 22:14–20,24–30; 23:32–43

A Final Meal with Friends

22:14 When the hour came, he took his place at the table, and the apostles with him. 15 He said to them, "I have eagerly desired to eat this Passover with you before I suffer; 16 for I tell you, I will not eat it until it is fulfilled in the kingdom of God." 17 Then he took a cup, and after giving thanks he said, "Take this and divide it among yourselves; 18 for I tell you that from now on I will not drink of the fruit of the vine until the kingdom of God comes."

19 Then he took a loaf of bread, and when he had given thanks, he broke it and gave it to them, saying, "This is my body, which is given for you. Do this in remembrance of me." 20 And he did the same with the cup after supper, saying, "This cup that is poured out for you is the new covenant in my blood." . . .

²⁴ A dispute also arose among them as to which one of them was to be regarded as the greatest. ²⁵ But he said to them, "The kings of the Gentiles lord it over them; and those in authority over them are called benefactors. ²⁶ But not so with you; rather the greatest among you must become like the youngest, and the leader like one who serves. ²⁷ For who is greater, the one who is at the table or the one who serves? Is it not the one at the table? But I am among you as one who serves.

²⁸ "You are those who have stood by me in my trials; ²⁹ and I confer on you, just as my Father has conferred on me, a kingdom, ³⁰ so that you may eat and drink at my table in my kingdom." . . .

The King and the Convict

²³:³² Two others also, who were criminals, were led away to be put to death with him. ³³ When they came to the place that is called The Skull, they crucified Jesus there with the criminals, one on his right and one on his left. ³⁴ Then Jesus said, "Father, forgive them; for they do not know what they are doing." And they cast lots to divide his clothing.

³⁵ And the people stood by, watching; but the leaders scoffed at him, saying, "He saved others; let him save himself if he is the Messiah of God, his chosen one!" ³⁶ The soldiers also mocked him, coming up and offering him sour wine, ³⁷ and saying, "If you are the King of the Jews, save yourself!" ³⁸ There was also an inscription over him, "This is the King of the Jews."

³⁹ One of the criminals who were hanged there kept deriding him and saying, "Are you not the Messiah? Save yourself and us!" ⁴⁰ But the other rebuked him, saying, "Do you not fear God, since you are under the same sentence of condemnation? ⁴¹ And we indeed have been condemned justly, for we are getting what we deserve for our deeds, but this man has done nothing wrong." ⁴² Then he said, "Jesus, remember me when you come into your kingdom." ⁴³ He replied, "Truly I tell you, today you will be with me in Paradise."

Questions for a Closer Look

1 What role does 22:27 suggest Jesus played at the Last Supper?

2 What qualities of a good teacher does Jesus display in 22:25–27? What do you suppose he was feeling?

3 Jesus directs his followers to keep on celebrating his last meal "in remembrance" of him (22:19). Do any of Jesus' statements suggest that celebrating the Lord's Supper should point our attention not only toward the past but also toward the future?

4 The second criminal undergoes a last-minute conversion (23:40–42). What do his words tell us about conversion?

A Guide to the Reading

In our readings so far, Jesus has announced by word and by deed that God's Kingdom is about to arrive. God's Kingdom, his loving care breaking into our lives, is a powerful reality. Jesus healed the sick and mixed with sinners to give people a taste of God's Kingdom (Week 2). His parables have illustrated the mercy of the Kingdom: the father of the two sons showed us what God's forgiveness is like (Week 3), and Lazarus being comforted in heaven reflected God's compassion for the poor (Week 4). Now Jesus made it possible for us to enter God's Kingdom—at the price of his own suffering and death.

The two scenes that we read are taken from Luke's account of Jesus' final hours. We read of Jesus' last meal and his execution, omitting the stories in between about his arrest, interrogation, and condemnation. It is a good idea to put the table and the cross side by side, like two photos in a hinged double frame, because the meal and the death are closely connected.

Jesus dies during the great Jewish feast of Passover. Passover celebrates the Israelites' Exodus, or going out, from slavery in Egypt. Now it will be Jesus who goes out, leaving this world by a painful death to enter into the majesty of God (9:28–31). He will do this in order to bring God's Kingdom to men and women. (Notice how Jesus connects his suffering with the coming of the kingdom in 22:15–18.)

Jesus uses ideas from the Old Testament to show what he will do through his death: his body will be given, and his blood poured out to form a new covenant, a bond, between God and us (22:19–20). How his death brings this about is something even the great saints and theologians cannot fully understand. Jesus simply tells his disciples that in God's plan it "must" be (9:22; 17:25; 22:37).

By using the Passover meal to explain the purpose of his death, Jesus turns the focus of the meal on himself. With the words "do this in remembrance of me" (22:19) Jesus re-creates the Passover meal as the sacrament of his presence. He speaks new words before the meal when the bread is broken and after the meal when the wine is blessed. Of the bread he declares, "This is my body, which is given for you"; of the cup, "This cup that is poured out for you is the new covenant in my blood" (22:19–20).

This means that Jesus' death will always be present to his followers in this meal, because he himself will be fully and truly present. Jesus is so present in the Eucharist, in fact, that when we celebrate it, we do not merely remember or repeat the Last Supper: we actually participate in it. In a sense, the altar in the church is the same table around which Jesus and his disciples ate the Last Supper.

The scene shifts to just outside the city, to a small hill called the Skull because of its shape (*Golgotha* in Aramaic, *Calvary* in Latin—23:33). Jesus had said that he mixed with sinners in order to show that God wanted to be reconciled with them. Now, at the Skull, Jesus continues this mission to his last breath, spending his final hours among criminals.

The religious leaders, the execution squad, and one of the criminals hanging next to Jesus ridicule him (23:35–37,39). They assume that if the Messiah were mistreated, he would save himself. They do not understand that the Messiah has come not to save himself but to save others.

Who can say how much the other criminal understands? But at least he has the humility to acknowledge his sins. He knows that he needs Jesus, and he is willing to put his trust in Jesus even though Jesus does not seem at this moment capable of helping anyone. The criminal understands somehow that the titles others are using to mock Jesus—"king," "Messiah" (23:35–39)—are true. Jesus really *is* the king sent by God (23:42).

When the convict appeals to Jesus to have mercy on him, the dying king tells him what we all hope to hear at the hour of our death (23:43). In fact, in talking with the man, Jesus shows the real reason for his life and death: to open the way for people to receive God's forgiveness, to gain a place for us at the joyous supper in the kingdom (22:30). To share that supper is the ultimate purpose of our lives.

Questions for Application

1 Jesus was under a great deal of stress at the Last Supper. What was Jesus' focus during this last meal with his friends? What can we learn from Jesus about dealing with stress during family meals?

2 The disciples do not seem to understand Jesus' call to serve (22:24). What are some of the ways in which we receive God's call to serve? What is Jesus calling us to do in 22:26?

3 Do you think it was easy for Jesus to pray for forgiveness for his enemies (23:34)? How can we best imitate him?

4 We believe that Jesus gave his life for us. How should that belief affect the way we live our lives?

5 People react differently to Jesus' death on the cross. What feelings do you have as you read about the crucifixion?

6 What can we learn from the repentant criminal's response to Jesus?

Approach to Prayer

Listen as a member of the group begins with this prayer:

> *Lord Jesus, like the repentant thief,*
> *I have nothing to offer you*
> *except my repentance and my*
> *faith in you. Like him, I appeal*
> *to you. Have mercy and remember*
> *me this day in your kingdom.*
> *Lord Jesus, you have given your*
> *life for me. Help me respond to*
> *you with my whole life.*

Then take a few moments to express to the Lord—either silently or aloud—the thoughts that are on your mind after the reading and discussion.

Finally pray along with the group Psalm 22, a prayer that foreshadowed Jesus' death. According to the Gospels of Matthew and Mark, this is the prayer that Jesus prayed on the cross.

A Living Tradition

The Repentant Thief

Here is the model of conversion that we should aim at, since forgiveness is instantly lavished on the thief, and he finds favor and friendship more abundant than he asked for—because the Lord always bestows more than we request. The thief asked the Lord to remember him when he came into his kingdom, but the Lord said, "I assure you, today you will be with me in paradise"(23:43). For life consists in being with Christ, because where Christ is, there is the kingdom. The reason the Lord pardoned the man so quickly was that the man so quickly turned to him.
Saint Ambrose of Milan

The thief acknowledged his sin, testified to Christ's innocence, believed in him, addressed him as king even though he was hanging on a cross. By all this he snatched for himself the inheritance of the saints.
Saint Cyril of Alexandria

My patron saints are those who have stolen heaven—like the good thief. The great saints have earned heaven by their works; as for me, I will imitate the thief, I will have it by ruse, a ruse of love, which will open heaven's gates to me and to poor sinners.
Saint Thérèse of Lisieux

Accept me as a partaker of your mystical supper, O Son of God,
for I will not reveal your mystery to your enemies, nor will I give
you a kiss as did Judas, but like the thief I confess to you:
Remember me, O Lord, when you come into your kingdom!
Remember me, O Master, when you come into your kingdom!
Remember me, O Holy One, when you come into your kingdom!
May the partaking of your holy mysteries, O Lord, be not for my
judgment or condemnation, but for the healing of soul and body.
Pre-communion prayer of the Byzantine liturgy

Between Discussions

L uke's description of the Last Supper and Jesus' crucifixion gives us plenty to think about. Here are two lines of reflection, one concerning the Eucharist, the other concerning the sacrament of reconciliation:

The Eucharist ~ The Passover meal was, and is, a celebration of God's mercy. The meal thanks God in the normal Old Testament manner by remembering what God had done, praising him for it, and telling other people about it. The Passover meal specifically recalls how God rescued the Israelites from slave labor and genocidal oppression in Egypt. At different points in the meal there are blessings in connection with wine and bread. It is not the food that is blessed, however, but God: God is blessed, that is, praised, over the food. So the whole meal is an expression of praise and thanks to God for what he has done. In the final blessing over the wine, there is another prayer of petition for the welfare of God's people, Israel.

Luke does not describe the entire Passover meal that Jesus ate with his disciples. He only records the words Jesus used to give the meal new meaning. In their liturgy, however, the early Christians did not merely repeat these few words of Jesus. They took the Passover meal and made it into a Christian celebration. So instead of recalling the Exodus, they gave thanks for the death and resurrection of Jesus, which bring freedom from sin and death. They also offered prayers of petition for God's people, the Church.

Eventually the meal was dropped, but the prayers remained. The Mass has changed over the centuries, but it has always remained faithful to the original elements. Today the Eucharistic prayer opens with praise and thanks to God for his goodness, above all for the death and resurrection of his Son. It quotes the words Jesus used to give the meal its new meaning centered on himself. And it concludes with prayers for God's people, the Church.

Seeing the connection between the Last Supper and our Mass helps us understand why the liturgical celebration is called the

Eucharist. The word *eucharist* comes from the Greek for "thanksgiving." The Christian liturgy is an act of thanksgiving because, ever since its origin in the Passover meal, it praises and thanks God for his ultimate saving action through Jesus.

The next time you are at Mass, pay attention to the eucharistic prayer (it begins with the exchange "Lift up your hearts," "We lift them up to the Lord"). Notice how the prayer is the great proclamation of thanks and praise to God for the saving action of his Son and the great prayer for the Church and the world. Do you actively take part in the whole celebration? Do you weave your heart and your voice into the responses and songs that make up the fabric of the Eucharist?

The Sacrament of Reconciliation ~ Jesus was strongly criticized for dining with tax collectors and sinners. The Gospel of Luke shows that Jesus' disciples also had their flaws. For example, they were ambitious and argued among themselves (9:46; 22:24). Jesus always sought the company of men and women who were far from holy.

Jesus showed his affection for imperfect people quite clearly at his final meal. He dined with faithless followers. One would betray him (22:21–22). Another would deny him (22:31–34). The rest would humiliate him by abandoning him. Yet Jesus told them, "I have eagerly desired to eat this Passover with you before I suffer" (22:15). He did not love people less because of their failings, even when their failings added to his suffering.

Jesus proved his love during his final hours. The shame and torture of his death would have uncovered any feelings of vengefulness he might have had. But at his crucifixion Jesus asked God to forgive those who were putting him to death (23:34). He was a man of mercy through and through.

Is this the Jesus you picture as you come to the Sacrament of Reconciliation?

The Lord Has Risen Indeed

Warm-Up Questions

1 Two disciples in this reading walk 14 miles in a day. What would you think if you were told to walk 14 miles in a day?
- ○ No problem. (Hey, I run that far.)
- ○ Sounds like a decent hike—if I were in shape.
- ○ I enjoy walking. But not 14 miles!
- ○ Walking is best with a friend.
- ○ I wish!

2 Has anyone said something to you recently that lifted you out of discouragement?

3 What was your most interesting conversation with a stranger while traveling?

4 How can it benefit us to entertain strangers?

What's Happened

Jesus hangs crucified for some time after speaking with the repentant criminal. Then, quoting a psalm, he cries out, "Father, into your hands I commend my spirit," and dies (23:46). Thus Jesus ends his life as he began it, calling God his Father and giving himself completely to his Father's purposes (2:49).

Several women who are followers of Jesus have stood off at a distance, watching him die. They continue to watch as one of Jesus' friends removes his body from the cross and places it in a tomb hewn out of a rock hillside. The women wish to dignify Jesus' burial with aromatic spices. But because it is late Friday afternoon and the Sabbath is about to begin, they return to their lodgings and observe the Jewish day of rest. As soon as they can on Sunday morning, however, they go back to the tomb where they saw Jesus' body laid, bringing the spices. To their astonishment, the tomb is empty.

Two men—evidently angels—appear and reproach the women for seeking "the living among the dead" (24:4–5). The angels remind the women that Jesus predicted both his death and his resurrection.

The women are terrified. They go to tell the male disciples what they have seen and heard. The men dismiss the women's report as nonsense, although Peter goes to investigate and discovers that the tomb is, in fact, empty.

THE READING

Luke 24:13–35

On the Road and at Table with Jesus Once Again

[13] Now on that same day two of them were going to a village called Emmaus, about seven miles from Jerusalem, [14] and talking with each other about all these things that had happened. [15] While they were talking and discussing, Jesus himself came near and went with them, [16] but their eyes were kept from recognizing him.

[17] And he said to them, "What are you discussing with each other while you walk along?"

They stood still, looking sad. [18] Then one of them, whose name was Cleopas, answered him, "Are you the only stranger in Jerusalem who does not know the things that have taken place there in these days?"

[19] He asked them, "What things?"

They replied, "The things about Jesus of Nazareth, who was a prophet mighty in deed and word before God and all the people, [20] and how our chief priests and leaders handed him over to be condemned to death and crucified him. [21] But we had hoped that he was the one to redeem Israel. Yes, and besides all this, it is now the third day since these things took place. [22] Moreover, some women of our group astounded us. They were at the tomb early this morning, [23] and when they did not find his body there, they came back and told us that they had indeed seen a vision of angels who said that he was alive. [24] Some of those who were with us went to the tomb and found it just as the women had said; but they did not see him."

[25] Then he said to them, "Oh, how foolish you are, and how slow of heart to believe all that the prophets have declared! [26] Was it not necessary that the Messiah should suffer these things and then enter into his glory?" [27] Then beginning with Moses and all the prophets, he interpreted to them the things about himself in all the scriptures.

[28] As they came near the village to which they were going, he walked ahead as if he were going on. [29] But they urged him strongly, saying, "Stay with us, because it is almost evening and the day is now nearly over." So he went in to stay with them. [30] When he was at the table with them, he took bread, blessed and broke it, and gave it to them. [31] Then their eyes were opened, and they recognized him; and he vanished from their sight.

[32] They said to each other, "Were not our hearts burning within us while he was talking to us on the road, while he was opening the scriptures to us?"

[33] That same hour they got up and returned to Jerusalem; and they found the eleven and their companions gathered together. [34] They were saying, "The Lord has risen indeed, and he has appeared to Simon!" [35] Then they told what had happened on the road, and how he had been made known to them in the breaking of the bread.

Questions for a Closer Look

1 Jesus seems to play ignorant in verse 19. Why?

2 Compare the meal described in verse 30 with the description of the Last Supper in the previous reading (22:14,19). How are they similar?

3 What does verse 32 suggest about what the disciples had experienced with Jesus in the past?

4 From glimpses of Jesus' disciples in this reading (especially in 24:13–15,22–24,33–35), what picture do you get of their relationships with one another?

5 Some people say that Jesus' disciples made up the story of his resurrection. What evidence against this theory can you find in the reading? (Consider 24:1–12 also.)

A Guide to the Reading

On the Sunday after Jesus' death, two of his followers are walking from Jerusalem to a nearby village, probably their hometown. One was named Cleopas (24:18), and a later tradition identified him as a brother of Joseph, Jesus' foster father. Cleopas' son later became a leader of the church in Jerusalem. Some scholars suggest that the unnamed companion may have been Cleopas' wife.

The two disciples had seen their expectations for Jesus shattered and they are extremely depressed. They had thought that they were about to witness God's decisive saving action in the world, when suddenly the person who was going to do this for God was destroyed by a ghastly execution.

Jesus comes up to the pair as they walk along, but they do not recognize him. This was not the only time when the disciples failed to recognize the resurrected Jesus at first (Matthew 28:17; John 20:14). He must have undergone an unbelievable transformation.

Jesus tells the pair that they do not understand God's plan (24:25). In a way, they are as misguided as the people who taunted Jesus at the cross. Those people had thought that the Messiah would use his great power to save himself. It had never occurred to them that the Messiah would bring about healing and reconciliation through his own suffering and death. Yet that is what Jesus explains to his two followers. God will work through a suffering Messiah—a plan God had sketched out beforehand in Scripture (24:26–27).

As they walked along, Jesus probably also set the disciples straight regarding their expectation that he would liberate Israel (24:21). Jesus is the savior of Israel, but not of Israel alone, and not from its political enemies. He has come forth from Israel to save both Jews and non-Jews from sin and to share with all people his own resurrection from death.

For the two disciples, these are revolutionary views. There was not much in the Judaism of that time to lead them to expect a suffering Messiah. Today we are used to the idea of a suffering

Messiah—a crucified Christ. But does that make it any easier to understand or respond to? How astonishing that God would bring his mercy to us through his Son's humiliating torment! And how hard it is for us to accept what that means for us. What it means is that the only way we can follow the suffering Messiah into his glory is for us to be humble like him, to serve and to suffer with him (see 9:23–27). It will be a lifetime challenge for us to follow the example of the suffering Messiah. (Remember that the first disciples had a hard time accepting this idea; for example, see 22:24–27.)

The disciples are so impressed with his surprising explanation of things that they ask him to stay for dinner (24:29). Jesus then reverses roles: invited in as a guest, he becomes the host. He says the blessing over the bread (24:30), and the disciples recognize him. Immediately he vanishes (24:31).

The two disciples have learned more from the afternoon's events than the bare fact that Jesus is risen. His explanation on the road has helped them understand that suffering has been his path into splendor and authority with God. They recognize him just at that moment when he repeats the action he performed at the Last Supper. This shows them that he will continue to be with them in the meal that he told his apostles to repeat, the meal that will make present his sacrificial death (compare 24:30 with 22:14,19). In this meal, he had declared, the bread and wine would become his body and blood (22:19–20). By his appearance at the meal at Emmaus, Jesus reveals the fulfillment of that promise. He shows that in the celebration of this meal he will continue to accompany his disciples and provide the strength they need to make their way into his glory.

Notice that Luke does not say that Jesus left but that he "vanished from their sight" (24:31). The point of the story is that, though Jesus is invisible, in the celebration of the Eucharist he remains with us in a way more real than we can understand.

Questions for Application

1 What is your understanding of the purpose of Jesus' death and resurrection? If Jesus has truly passed through suffering and death into risen life, what effect should this have on your life?

2 What do verses 24:25–27, and 32 tell us about what Scripture ought to mean in our lives today? ("Moses and all the prophets"—24:27—refers to what Christians call the Old Testament.) What place does Scripture have in your life?

3 What elements of faith are perhaps the hardest for young people to believe (see 24:25)? What might they do to strengthen their faith?

4 How can this reading help someone who is feeling discouraged over something in his or her life?

5 How has the Lord shown you the reality of his presence? What effect did this experience have on you? What effect does it have on you now?

6 What is the most important thing you are going to take away from these readings and discussions of Luke? What is the most important response to Jesus that Luke's Gospel invites you to make?

Approach to Prayer

Listen as a member of the group reads the opening prayer:

We thank you, Lord Jesus, for your presence
with us during our reading of the Gospel of Luke.
Thank you for your words to us, which you have
spoken to us by your Spirit, through the Gospel
and through one another. Help us respond to the words
you have spoken to each of us. Lord, let it be done to us
according to your word!

Reflect quietly for a moment on how you will respond to what
God has given you through the readings and discussions.

End by praying Mary's prayer with the group (1:46–55).

Saints in the Making

Luke's First Readers

With one exception (see 1:3), we do not know the names of Luke's first readers. But at least a few of them seem to have been materially well off. Luke's writing is rather sophisticated and seems designed for people who had the time and resources to get a good education. Luke preserves many sayings of Jesus that are particularly aimed at people who have wealth (for example, the story of the rich man and Lazarus).

People of lower social standing also belonged to the early Christian communities, and some of them must have been very poor. Besides slaves, there were free unskilled laborers, who were hired one day at a time and earned enough to live on for the next day. If one day they did not get work, the next day they did not eat.

The pagan culture they were raised in showed little concern for the poor, and so wealthy Christians may not have been very generous with their poorer brothers and sisters. (First Corinthians 11:17–22 offers evidence of such a problem.) But many well-off converts to Christianity *did* learn a new way of relating to the poor. The writings of the early Church make many references to the regular collections taken up for widows, orphans, and the elderly.

Moreover, in Luke's time Christians celebrated the Eucharist in the home of a community member who was wealthy enough to provide space for a meeting. This made the Eucharist an exceptional gathering, for it was the only time that both rich and poor would come together to associate with each other.

The result was that, if you were someone from the upper class and you wanted to live the Gospel of Luke, you had to give away not just some of your money but also some of your social respectability. The Christians who were willing to follow Jesus this way were, indeed, saints in the making.

After Words

I t is difficult to leave our discussion of Emmaus without a few additional reflections.

On the road to Emmaus, Jesus showed the disciples how Scripture points to him. Then he breaks bread with them. Luke's readers would immediately have recognized that they did the same thing in their celebration of the Eucharist: read and preach on Scripture and then unite with the risen Lord in the breaking of the bread. We still do the same thing as Emmaus in our Mass, which consists of a Liturgy of the Word and a Liturgy of the Eucharist. Our Christian worship is based on Jesus' actions with his disciples at Emmaus. Indeed, it is a continuation of Jesus' actions. Every time we celebrate the Eucharist, we share in Jesus' meal at Emmaus, just as we share in the Last Supper.

There are, in fact, a number of connections between the Last Supper and the Emmaus meal. At the Last Supper, Jesus told his disciples to celebrate a meal remembering his death, and that through that meal he would continue to be present with them under the appearances of bread and wine. At Emmaus, after explaining his saving death, Jesus shows his disciples that he is indeed with them in the breaking of the bread. The Last Supper was a farewell before departure; the Emmaus meal was a resumption of life together, a "remaining with" meal.

If we put these two meals together with the other meals described in Luke and the Acts of the Apostles (which Luke also wrote), we see that they are part of a larger pattern. There is a series of meals leading up to Jesus' death and resurrection, then a series of meals following his death and resurrection. The pattern looks like this:

➤ From Galilee to Jerusalem Jesus practiced table fellowship with all sorts of men and women, gathering them into a new community of God's people. These meals reached a climax at the Last Supper, when Jesus gave himself to his friends completely in a meal that already made present his saving death and resurrection.

➤ Jesus suffered, died, and rose to new life.

➤ Jesus celebrated a kind of First Supper with his friends at Emmaus. In this meal he made his crucified and glorified self present to them. This new meal now continues on in Christian celebrations of the Eucharist, in which Jesus gathers all sorts of men and women into a renewed community of God's people centered on himself. Here is where we fit in. As we join in the Eucharist, we hear Jesus teach and we dine with him, like the disciples at Emmaus. We have access to his mercy as did the people who approached him when he was traveling from town to town in Galilee and sharing meals with them.

The celebration of the Lord's Supper will stretch on to the end of time, when the Kingdom of God comes fully. When we celebrate, we participate in Jesus' death and resurrection, which have already taken place, and in their fulfillment, which will take place at the end of time. Jesus spoke of God's Kingdom as a great banquet (14:15–24), and he established a connection between his Last Supper and that banquet (22:16,18). When we unite with him in eating and drinking the Eucharist, our eating and drinking is already a sharing in the Final Supper of his Kingdom that will come.

As we conclude our study of the Gospel of Luke, we might ask ourselves what happiness we are seeking. Would we be happy if we attained it? Do we know what will really make us happy?

Luke shows us that sharing in God's happiness means becoming people who are interested in the happiness of others. To receive God's mercy means becoming people who show mercy. Are we willing to undergo that change?

Mercy and More Mercy

Sister Inez Raymond was a teacher in a junior high school. Like all other teachers, she had many different kinds of students, but one of her outstanding features was that she liked every single student in her class. Her students never crossed swords with her.

This does not mean that Sister Inez had a rowdy class. Her students respected her. More than other teachers she used games to make learning fun, but she was serious about her students' learning. Sister Inez had a high estimate of what they were capable of, and she did not rest until they achieved it. Her individual affection for each student made it hard to escape her searching attention. Hers was not a class where you could easily hide your lack of effort in the crowd.

Most of us have probably had a Sister Inez or two in our past—a teacher who combined deep kindness with high expectations. From reading the Gospel of Luke, one might be inclined to think that Jesus was something like Sister Inez—or that she was a little like him. Luke shows us Jesus being almost too merciful, yet at the same time demanding a great deal of people. People like Sister Inez may help us understand how Jesus could be both merciful and demanding.

One way in which Jesus showed mercy was by dining in the homes of "tax collectors and sinners." Twice in our selected readings people criticize Jesus for doing this (5:30; 15:2). The reproach followed Jesus through his public life (7:34; 19:7). The criticism makes sense once you understand who tax collectors and sinners were. Tax collectors were not government employees. They were independent agents with whom the government contracted to collect the tolls. These collectors were backed with police enforcement. They took much more from people than the people owed the government, and then the tax collector kept the difference. Tax collectors made a lot of money but not many friends. They were as unpopular as gangsters.

Sinners is a broader group. Jews who strictly observed certain portions of the Mosaic law sometimes applied the term *sinners* to Jews who did not keep those portions like they did. But *sinners* also had a more serious application. In the Old Testament the word *sinners* meant "the wicked." The wicked were those who looked for ways to take land away from the poor, mistreated widows and orphans, destroyed others' reputations by spreading lies about them, even plotted their neighbors' murder (for example, see Psalm 10).

How could a religious reformer possibly cultivate friendships with such people? Yet Jesus did, and what is surprising about his doing so is that he always talked about showing mercy to the poor—yet tax collectors and sinners were people who mistreated the poor. Jesus announced good news for the poor and release for the oppressed (4:17–21)—yet tax collectors were the biggest oppressors around. Every time they imposed an extra tax on shipments of flour or dates, it meant that the poor had to pay more money for their food. Men like Zacchaeus became wealthy by working the tax system to their advantage (19:2,8). They were the exact opposite of the poor, whom Jesus proclaimed blessed in the Kingdom of God. Jesus shocked people by eating with the tax collectors and sinners in the same way that a preacher in the Confederate South might proclaim the Gospel to slaves in the cotton field and then have dinner at the plantation owner's mansion.

How can we understand Jesus' friendships with both the exploited and their exploiters? It may be that Jesus saw the tax collectors and sinners as also, in some sense, poor. Not that Jesus did not understand what it really meant to be poor. The Greek word for the poor in Luke's Gospel literally means "beggars," and that is clearly how Jesus intended it. Lazarus was, precisely, a beggar. But Jesus recognized that there is another way to be poor: we can be poor in our relationship with God, and we can be socially poor when we are rejected by other people. He felt a deep compassion for people who were poor in any sense. His compassion for the materially poor did not make him less compassionate for those people who, while materially wealthy, were poor spiritually and socially.

Jesus loved tax collectors and sinners deeply. He did not dine only with those who were sorry for what they had done. He dined also with people who had difficulty accepting his message. After all, if the tax collectors had always accepted his message and changed their ways, everybody would have applauded Jesus rather than criticized him. People who bought taxed goods would have loved to see the tax collectors repent. The fact that people continued to complain about Jesus' friendships with tax collectors throughout his public life suggests that he remained friends with those who did not change right away.

Thus Luke says that there were no limits to Jesus' mercy. This does not mean that Jesus had a relaxed attitude toward sin. Jesus took sin just as seriously as his opponents, the Jewish religious leaders. When he explains his program of friendship with sinners, he makes it clear that the heavenly rejoicing over those who return to God commences when they repent (15:7,10; see 7:36–50). For Jesus, mercy means forgiving sins, not overlooking them or rationalizing them away.

In fact, Jesus actually demanded more of people morally. He taught us to love our enemies (6:27). He taught us to deny ourselves, take up our crosses, and follow him (9:23). Jesus demands more than rule keeping. He asks for perfection.

If Jesus is both merciful and demanding, what does this mean for those of us who seek to follow him?

For one thing, we can draw hope from Jesus' friendships with tax collectors and sinners, for it shows that he loves us without conditions. His love for us is not based on how good we are or how well we are responding to his message. He loves us before we have a chance to say yes or no to him, in order to lead us to a positive response. He loves us even when we hesitate to respond, even when we put it off.

Furthermore, the perfection Jesus demands is essentially a perfection of mercy. He calls us to become perfect in giving to others what he gives to us. He calls us to humble ourselves and become the servants of others, just as he humbled himself and became our servant (22:24–27).

Finally, we can be encouraged by Luke's portrait of a Jesus who was both merciful and demanding with his disciples. There is no doubt that Jesus challenged them to be uncompromising in their forgiveness, mercy, and service. Yet there were no hard feelings in his correction of their shortcomings. When the disciples show that they are more interested in worldly greatness than in humble service, Jesus sets them straight without fussing at them (9:46–48). When they keep on being selfish, even when Jesus himself is under tremendous pressure, he corrects them mildly and adds words of encouragement (22:24–30). Jesus comes across as a patient, merciful teacher of the way of mercy.

Many of us may feel burdened by Jesus' call to perfection. We know that we fall far short of what he asks, and we feel bad about it. It is hard for us to conceive that he can be very happy with us because we know how poorly we do so often. We might feel discouraged sometimes and be tempted to give up or to measure ourselves by a lesser standard so that we will feel OK about ourselves and have a sense that Jesus is pleased with us. This would involve persuading ourselves that our sins are not so bad (or perhaps are not really sins at all), that our selfishness is not really a problem.

We would do better to accept Jesus as Luke portrays him, with both his high expectations and his limitless mercy. Judged according to his standard, "Be merciful, just as your Father is merciful" (6:36), we can only admit that we are still far from being what he expects. But then, our failure does not diminish his love for us. Our falling short will not stop him from inviting himself to dinner in our home. He will continue to offer his friendship in heartfelt love, for he wants what is best for us even more than we do.

A Young Person's Gospel

All four Gospels tell us important things that we need to know in order to live full lives as human beings and followers of Jesus Christ. But one or the other Gospel may be more meaningful to us at one time or another, and I think that, as a young person, you ought to regard Luke as your special Gospel. I say this because Luke's Gospel is the only one that addresses a rather full range of issues that young people face.

Luke, for example, is the only Gospel writer to address the issue of parent-child relationships in a story from Jesus' own adolescence (2:41–52). Jesus had gone down with his parents to Jerusalem to celebrate the feast of Passover. He was 12 years old, and he got separated somehow from his parents when it was time to return home. His poor parents looked for him frantically for four days, and they finally found him in the temple, calmly conversing with teachers. They were understandably upset, but he did not express any sorrow for what he had done. He did, however, go back with them to Nazareth, and Luke says that he "was obedient to them." After they got back to Nazareth, "Jesus advanced in wisdom and age and favor before God and man."

Jesus had reached the point in his life where he would begin striking out on his own. Like any young person, he is beginning to make his own decisions, and like any young person's parents, Mary and Joseph are going to suffer anxiety over some of those decisions. Jesus knew that he did not have to apologize for growing up, but he also understood the importance of maintaining a healthy relationship with his parents. He returned home and continued growing up under their loving care. And if Joseph and Mary watched him a little closer after this incident, we can understand why.

Luke has another story in which he takes up the issue of a young person's relationship with his or her parents. It is a story you have read earlier, the parable of the forgiving Father (15:11–32). The young son takes everything his father gives him and then leaves home. He seems to have made several mistakes. For one thing, he obviously took on more responsibilities than he could handle. Some of us do that in our youth: we think we are old enough to confront certain challenges, and we are not. But the son's biggest mistake seems to have been his cutting himself off from his father. From all that we know in the story, the father was a wonderful, loving man. There is no reason to believe that he drove his son out of the house.

Of course, there is that other son, the older one, the one who does not leave home but works obediently for his father. He, too, has problems with his father, but they are of a different kind. His problem is that he feels unappreciated. The father obviously loves this son, and he even goes out into the field to try to talk him into joining the party. But maybe the son was right, and maybe the father did not show him enough appreciation.

Or maybe the real problem the older son was experiencing was not with his father but rather with his little brother. Here, again, Luke is addressing an issue of concern to many young people: the challenge of dealing with brothers and sisters. One might criticize the older brother for being jealous of his brother, but I can understand his feelings. The younger son was probably a difficult brother to get along with, and he may very well have been a spoiled child. The father is caught in the middle, and we can only hope that he encouraged the younger son to make up with his big brother. Luke's story does not settle all these issues for us, but it does encourage us to address sibling relationships seriously and within the context of a loving family.

Luke is also the only Gospel writer to directly take up the issue of going to school. He does it in a story about two women named Martha and Mary (10:38–42). The two sisters had welcomed Jesus into their home, and Martha busied herself around the house, preparing things for him and making sure he was well taken care of. Mary, on the other hand, "sat beside the Lord at his feet listening to him speak." What you need to know is that young people went to school in those days by sitting at the feet of a teacher and learning from him. We can say that Jesus was "going to school" when he was in the Temple in Jerusalem. Now Mary is "going to school," and her sister wants her to get up and do some work. Jesus defends Mary and says that what she is doing is right. The work can come later, Jesus seems to be saying. Right now Mary needs to educate herself, and that is what she ought to do. It is not always easy to stick to our education, but it is what we ought to do.

Luke also has two stories about the health and well-being of young people (8:40–56; 9:37–43). In the first story a 12-year old girl is dying, and her father comes to Jesus to ask for his help. By the time Jesus got there, she was already dead. But Jesus "took her by the hand and called to her, 'Child, arise!' Her breath returned and she immediately arose." In the other story, a man asks Jesus to look at his son, an only child. "For a spirit seizes him and he suddenly screams and it convulses him until he foams at the mouth; it releases him only with difficulty, wearing him out." Luke tells us that Jesus "rebuked the unclean spirit, healed the boy, and returned him to his father."

In both stories it is clear that Jesus is concerned for the young people. He wants them to be alive and well. We know from other healing stories that Jesus would forgive the sins of those he healed, letting them know that he wanted them to be healthy in every way. Jesus no doubt wanted these young people also to be healthy in every way. He made them physically strong, but he wanted them to be healthy psychologically and socially, to have no moral illnesses, to be spiritually well. His concern was for the total person, and we can hope that the two young people he made well grew up to be happy, well-adjusted adults.

Finally, there is a small passage in Luke that impresses upon us the importance of youth. "People were bringing even infants to him that he might touch them, and when the disciples saw this, they rebuked them. Jesus, however, called the children to himself and said, 'Let the children come to me and do not prevent them; for the kingdom of God belongs to such as these. Amen, I say to you, whoever does not accept the kingdom of God like a child will not enter it'" (18:15–17). The young people were very important to Jesus, and indeed they represented something that he was trying to teach his disciples about. Young people are willing to trust God. They are open to new ideas and new approaches, and they are anxious to learn. They tend to look on the brighter side of things, and they want to enjoy life. All of that seemed to fit into Jesus' idea of what God has in mind for us. You are all going to have to be that way in order to enter the Kingdom of God.

In this last story and in all of his Gospel, Luke seems to be making the point that youth is an important part of a person's life, and that Jesus was very anxious that this part of life be lived well. Perhaps as you read the rest of Luke's Gospel, you will find more messages that seem to be addressed to you as a young person, for there can be no doubt that both Jesus and Luke were concerned for your well-being and happiness as a young person.

Listening When God Speaks

As you have worked your way through this book, you have been listening to God's word. But this is not the first time that God has spoken to you, and indeed God has been speaking to you throughout your young life. Let's look at some of the ways in which God speaks to you, and let's look at some of the ways in which you can improve your listening skills.

The most obvious way in which you receive messages from God is through the Scripture, which is the Word of God. The people of Israel and the early Christians recorded their experiences of God's saving acts in history, and our religious tradition accepts their writings as God's Word to us. We believe that when we read Scripture, or hear it read, God is communicating his Word to us. It would be a good thing for you to develop the habit of reading the Bible on a regular basis, and you should make every effort to benefit from the weekly reading of Scripture at Mass.

An excellent way in which to listen to God speaking to us in Scripture is to pray the Scripture. Begin by adopting a proper prayer *posture* through the selection of an appropriate time and place for prayer. Once in the proper posture, become aware of God's *presence* in your life and in the time and place you have chosen for your prayer. Then *pray* for guidance from the Holy Spirit, asking help to understand the passage you will be reading and reflecting on. You are now ready to read your selected *passage,* but you must read slowly and deliberately, with the intention of hearing God's voice in the passage. After you have read and reread the passage, *pause* for reflection on the passage. Allow time for God to speak to you through the words of the text.

The Bible is the Word of God, but it is not the only Word of God. Jesus Christ is also the Word of God, the Word made flesh. The Gospel of John begins with that message: "In the beginning was the Word, and the Word was with God, and the Word was

God. . . . And the Word became flesh and made his dwelling among us." We want, then, to listen to God speaking to us in Jesus Christ and one good way to do that is by participating fully in Mass. Gathering together with the other worshipers, we enter into communion with them and with the presiding priest. The words and actions of the celebration put our spirits at rest, so that by the time we enter into communion with Christ in the Eucharist, we are in a position to hear God's message of love, peace, and salvation. We should not make the mistake of thinking that Jesus speaks to us only at the moment of receiving the Eucharist. His voice can be heard—if only we listen—through the community, through the priest, through the entire Eucharistic celebration, and finally, bringing it all together, in the eating and drinking of the Body and Blood of Christ.

Because the Church is the Body of Christ, we can also speak of the Church as the Word of God. God speaks to us through the community of believers, and in a special way through the leadership of that community. One way to listen to the voice of God in the Church is by paying attention to the voices of the believers nearest us: our parents and teachers, our parish priest, and the people we worship with on Sunday. Another way is to stay in touch with what the leadership of our Church is teaching. The bishops of our Church, especially the bishop of Rome, the Holy Father, and our own local bishop, the leader of the Church where we are active, speak to us in words that have the authority of the Word of God, and as Catholics we hear in them the voice of God.

Finally, God speaks to us in our own life experiences. The Second Vatican Council recovered the biblical image of "reading the signs of the times," that is, hearing the voice of God in the events of history. On the personal level, we can hear God speaking to us in such things as our encounters with others, our decisions, our successes and failures, and the challenges arising from the difficulties of life. To hear God's voice in our life experiences, we need to pay attention to those experiences, reflect on them, and learn from them.

There is a wonderful story in the Old Testament about a young boy named Samuel. (You can read it in 1 Samuel 3.) Samuel was assisting an old priest named Eli, who was waiting in the temple for God to speak to him. One night while he was sleeping, Samuel heard someone call him. He assumed it was Eli, so he went and woke Eli up to find out what he wanted. Eli responded that he had not called, and he sent the boy back to bed. After a while Samuel heard his name called again, but once more Eli told the boy that it was not him. When it happened a third time, Eli knew that it was God calling to Samuel and he said to the boy, "Go to sleep, and if you are called, reply, 'Speak, LORD, for your servant is listening.'"

The first thing to notice about this story is that everybody expected God to speak to the old priest, but God spoke to the young boy instead. It is important that you be receptive in your youth to the voice of God and not think that God will only speak to you "later." God is speaking to you now—in the Scriptures, in Jesus Christ, in the Church, and in your life experiences.

The other point of the story is that, in order to hear God speaking to us, we must be listening. Samuel would never have received God's message if he had not listened, and the same thing applies to us. Ours is a busy life, with plenty of noise. We need to learn how to cut through all the noise and listen to God speaking to us.

Resources

Bibles

The following editions of the Bible contain the full set of biblical books recognized by the Catholic Church, along with a great deal of useful explanatory material:

➤ The Catholic Youth Bible (Saint Mary's Press), which can be ordered with either the New American Bible or the New Revised Standard Version

➤ Student Bible for Catholics (Thomas Nelson Publishers), which uses the text of the New American Bible

➤ The Catholic Study Bible (Oxford University Press), which uses the text of the New American Bible

➤ The Catholic Bible: Personal Study Edition (Oxford University Press), which also uses the text of the New American Bible

Additional Sources

➤ Kodell, Jerome. *Gospel According to Luke.* Collegeville, MN: Liturgical Press, 1985.

➤ Singer-Towns, Brian. "Luke's Gospel," *Youth Update,* Cincinnati, OH: St. Anthony Messenger Press, December 2003.